Excel 365 - Part 2

Very easy introduction for beginners of all age groups

A step-by-step instruction containing 440 images

Book number: B2

For Windows

Author: Peter Kynast

Imprint

Bibliographic information published by the Deutsche Nationalbibliothek. The Deutsche Nationalbibliothek lists this publication in the Deutsche Nationalbibliografie; detailed bibliographic data is available on the Internet at http://dnb.dnb.de.

ityco
Easy computer books
Peter Kynast
Hochstraße 14
33615 Bielefeld
Germany

Phone: +49 521 61846
Internet: www.ityco.com
Email: info@ityco.com

Image credit
stock.adobe.com - Image number: 334675299 - deagreez

103

ISBN: 979-8-32635578-2
Independently Published

First edition, May 2024, © Peter Kynast

Introduction

Dear reader,

Welcome to Excel 365 Part 2!

If you already completed Excel 365 Part 1, this book is the perfect continuation for you. This book is also ideal for users that have been working with Excel for a long time and are confident in using the sum function and basic arithmetic operations but have not had any contact with the absolute references (dollar sign), percentage calculations or the MIN, MAX and average functions. These topics are part of the basic knowledge of Excel and are covered in detail in this book.

To make learning as easy as possible for you, the exercises are, as always, described step by step and supplemented with lots of pictures. Using practical examples, I will show you many new functions, important working techniques and the necessary basic knowledge for your successful work with Microsoft Excel.

This book is self-explanatory and the language is easy to understand - that is a promise! There are also repetitions built into the instructions. This will make it easy for you to memorize the new knowledge quickly. In this way, you will experience many successes and have an easy time learning Microsoft Excel.

Now I wish you lots of fun and success with Excel 365!

Best regards

P. Kynast

Peter Kynast

PS: If you like this book, I recommend that you continue with the third part of this Excel introduction, which will release in summer 2024.

Table of contents

Section 1

Instructions

Contents of this section:

- general information
- downloading sample files
- functions: MIN, MAX and AVERAGE
- creating references using the pointing method
- moving cells
- Auto Fill Options
- AutoSum button

1   General information

Please read the following notes on this book carefully.

1.1   Prerequisites

To work with this book, your computer should be equipped with Microsoft Windows 10 or 11 and Excel 365. ***Excel 365 - Part 1*** is the ideal preparation for this. Basic knowledge of Microsoft Windows is required.

1.2   Target audience

This book is a guide for self-learning and for Excel training courses. It is aimed at people who want to learn Excel from scratch and are looking for a simple and safe introduction.

1.3   Contents

- functions for determining average, largest and smallest values
- moving cells, rows and columns
- inserting and deleting rows and columns
- alternative input methods for formulas
- calculating with percentages, dates and times
- basics of cell contents and cell formats
- linking cells

- preventing references from being changed when filling cells (absolute references, dollar sign)
- applying important automatic corrections
- calculating totals using a button
- helpful working techniques
- keyboard shortcuts
- tips and tricks and much more

1.4   Structure

This book consists of 5 sections and 27 chapters. Sections 1 to 4 contain 16 step-by-step instructions with precise directions. Each mouse click is described in detail and almost always illustrated. At the end of each section, you will find an exercise that allows you to directly apply what you have learned. Section 4 is dedicated to recognizing and correcting errors. Section 5 goes into more detail on the basics and provides you with further explanations of sections 1 to 4.

1.5   Repetitions

New topics are described in detail several times in this book and illustrated clearly. After a few repetitions, the procedure is assumed to be familiar and is therefore only reproduced in abbreviated form. Pictures are reduced in size or omitted completely.

1.6   Highlighting

Emphasized terms are <u>underlined</u> or shown in ***bold and italics***. Comments on individual work steps are introduced with one of the following terms:

Attention: Indicates a possible problem.
Example: Describes an example.
Result: Explains the change that occurs because of the current work step.
Advice: Provides further explanations and information.
Or: Shows another, equivalent way.
Read more: Refers to a chapter with further explanations.

2   Instruction: Downloading sample files

You will need the corresponding sample files for the following instructions. You can download them from the ityco website. These instructions describe this process.

2.1   Instruction

2.1.1   Opening browser

1.   Open the browser of your choice, e.g. **Edge, Chrome** or **Firefox**.

Advice: Edge is used in this instruction because it is most likely already installed on your computer alongside Windows. However, this process can also be carried out with any other browser.

2.1.2   Opening the ityco website

2.   Enter the address **www.ityco.com** into the address bar.

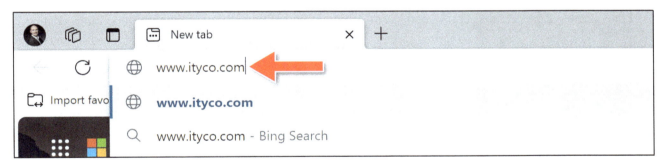

3.   Press the **enter key** ⏎ to open the website.

2.1.3   Downloading sample files

4.   Click on the **Files** button to open the page with the sample files.

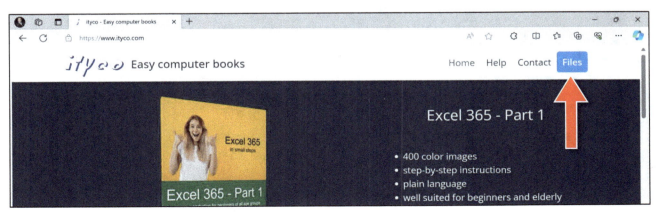

5. Scroll to the book **Excel 365 - Part 2 - B2** to access the sample files of this book.

Excel 365 – Part 2 – B2 ⬅

Chapter 03 – Wardrobe – Start – B2
Chapter 03 – Wardrobe – Result – B2
Chapter 04 – Temperatures – Start – B2
Chapter 04 – Temperatures – Result – B2
Chapter 05 – Clothing – Start – B2
Chapter 05 – Clothing – Result – B2
Chapter 06 – Butchery – Start – B2
Chapter 06 – Butchery – Result – B2
Chapter 07 – Data usage – Start – B2
Chapter 07 – Data usage – Result – B2

---

6. Scroll down slightly further until you see the link **Excel 365 - Part 2 - B2 - Download all sample files as a ZIP file**. Click on this link to download the file.

Chapter 21 – Currency conversion – Start – B2
Chapter 21 – Currency conversion – Result – B2
Chapter 22 – Devices – Start – B2
Chapter 22 – Devices – Result – B2

Excel 365 – Part 2 – B2 – Download all sample files as a ZIP file ⬅

Result: The file is downloaded and stored inside the **Downloads** folder.
Attention: Are you using Firefox? A window <u>may</u> appear asking whether you want to open the file directly or save it first. Select the **Save file** option here. Otherwise, you may have problems finding the file again later.

7. Click on the **Close** button [×] to close the browser.

8. Click on the yellow folder icon 📁 on the taskbar to open the **Explorer**.

Or: Press the keyboard shortcut **Windows** [⊞] + [E] to open the Explorer.
Advice: The Explorer gives you access to files and folders on your computer. Explorer is therefore the most important app for your daily work.

9. Click on the **Downloads** folder to open it.

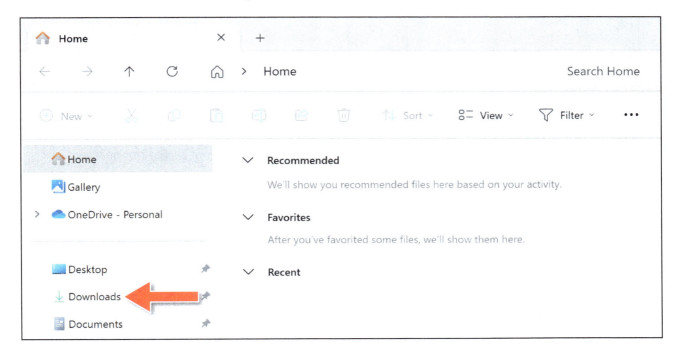

2.1.4   Unpacking ZIP files

The sample files are bundled in a so-called ZIP file. This combining is also called zipping or packing. To work with the sample files, you should unzip the ZIP file first. Unpacking is also known as unzipping or extracting.

10. Look at the downloaded ZIP file.

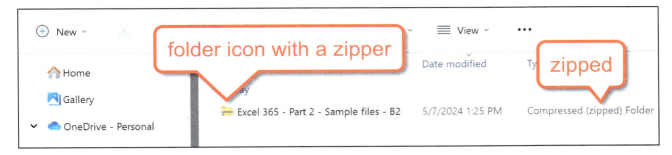

Advice: ZIP files are displayed as a folder icon with a zipper. You can see the **Compressed (zipped) Folder** description in the **Type** column.

11. Right-click on the ZIP file to open the context menu.

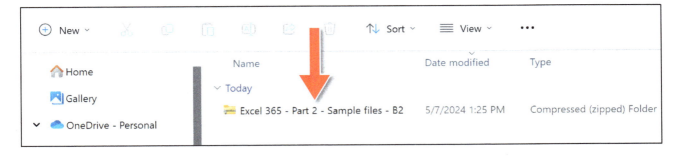

12. Click on the **Extract All** list item in the context menu to start extracting (unzipping).

Result: The **Extract Compressed (Zipped) Folders** dialog box is displayed.

13. Click on the **Show extracted files when complete** checkbox to disable this option.

Advice: Extracting creates another folder. It contains the extracted sample files. If this box is checked when extracting, this folder will be opened automatically.

14. Click on the **Extract** button to start the extraction.

Result: The ZIP file is extracted (unzipped). The **Extract Compressed (Zipped) Folders** dialog box is then closed automatically.

15. Look at the result. You may need to scroll with the mouse to see the extracted sample file folder.

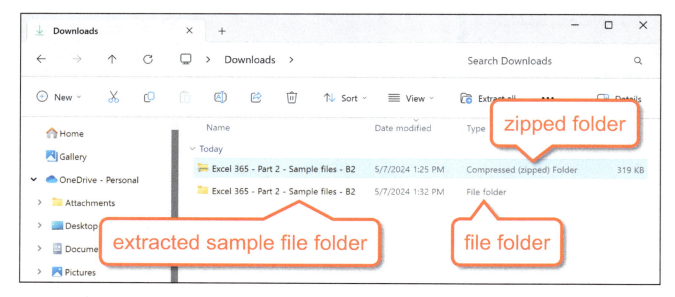

2.1.5   Deleting the ZIP file

The ZIP file and the folder are only slightly different. It is therefore advisable to delete the ZIP file. This way you avoid confusion when working through the exercises. If you wish, you can download the ZIP file from the website again at any time.

16. Right-click on the ZIP file.

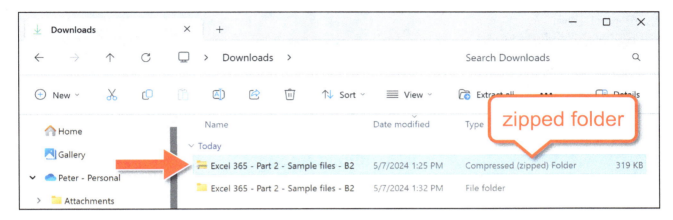

17. Click on the **Delete** button to delete the ZIP file.

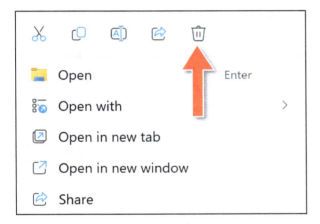

Attention: If you are working with Windows 10, the **Delete** command is not displayed as a recycling bin icon, but as a word in the list instead.

18. Close the **Explorer** and continue with the next chapter.

Do you need help?

Do you have any questions about this book or Excel? Write us an email and we will be happy to help you personally! Please also look at our homepage on the Internet. We have prepared some help topics for you there.

Email: info@ityco.com

Internet: www.ityco.com → Help

3 Instruction: Wardrobe

Use these instructions to calculate the billing amount for a wardrobe. The result of the table is shown on the right.

3.1 New content

- moving cells
- zooming with the mouse
- inserting cell references by clicking on them

3.2 Repetitions

- simple formulas

3.3 Instruction

	A	B	C
1	Wardrobe		
2	Retail price	$ 1,800.00	
3	Floor model discount	$ 200.00	
4	Subtotal	$ 1,600.00	
5	Delivery	$ 59.00	
6	**Billing amount**	**$ 1,659.00**	
7			

Result: Wardrobe

3.3.1 Start

1. Open the sample file *Chapter 03 - Wardrobe - Start - B2*.
   Read more: The instructions for downloading the sample files can be found in chapter 2, page 3.
2. Click on the *Enable editing* button at the top right of the ribbon.

Result: The workbook can now be edited.
Attention: This message does not always appear. If you do not see the button, you can already edit the file.

3.3.2 Moving cells

There is an error in this table. Cell A8 should be moved to A7.

3. Select Cell A8. Point the mouse anywhere on the frame of the cell pointer. However, do not point to the fill handle.

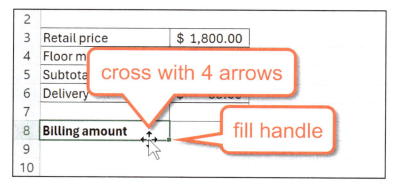

cross with 4 arrows

fill handle

Result: The mouse pointer is displayed with a cross consisting of four arrows .

Advice: The mouse pointer symbolizes the moving of cells. In contrast, the fill handle is only used to fill cells, but not to move them.

4. Hold down the left mouse button and drag the mouse to cell A7.

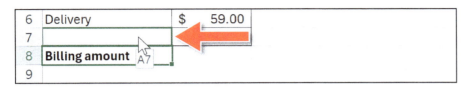

Advice: The wide green frame symbolizes the new position of the cell.

5. Release the mouse button.

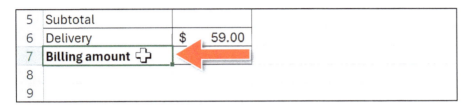

Result: The content of A8 is moved to cell A7. The formats are also transferred from A8 to A7.

3.3.3   Zooming with the mouse

The standard zoom factor of an Excel worksheet is 100 %. The zoom factor shows the size of the worksheet. You can read and change this value at the bottom right of the program window. It is easier and quicker to change this value using the mouse.

6. Press and hold the ***control key*** Ctrl .
7. Turn the mouse wheel forwards to increase the ***zoom factor***. Pay attention to the zoom factor in the right-hand area of the Excel Status bar.

Result: The zoom factor is increased in steps of ***15 %***.

8. Hold down the ***control key*** Ctrl and turn the mouse wheel forwards until the zoom factor is set to ***130 %***.
    Advice: The zoom factor has been chosen arbitrarily in this situation. You can also select a different value. The zoom factor has <u>no</u> effect on the printout. It is a change in the size of your table that can only be seen on the screen.

3.3.4   Insert cell references into formulas by clicking on them (point method)

Cell references can be inserted into a formula in various ways. In Excel Part 1, you entered all cell references manually using the keyboard. In the following steps, you will insert cell references by clicking on a cell. You do not need to read the name of the cell beforehand. This procedure is often faster and safer, especially with large tables. This method is also called the pointing method

9. Select cell B5 and enter an equal sign (=).

4	Floor model discount	$	200.00
5	Subtotal	=	
6	Delivery	$	59.00

10. Click on cell B3 with the mouse to insert the cell reference.

2			
3	Retail price	$ 1,800.00	*mouse*
4	Floor model discount	$ 200.00	
5	Subtotal	=B3	*cell reference*
6	Delivery	$ 59.00	

Result: The cell reference of B3 is automatically entered into the formula.

11. Enter a minus sign (-) using the keyboard.

2			
3	Retail price	$ 1,800.00	
4	Floor model discount	$ 200.00	
5	Subtotal	=B3-	*minus*
6	Delivery	$ 59.00	

12. Click on cell B4 with the mouse to inert the cell reference.

2			
3	Retail price	$ 1,800.00	*mouse*
4	Floor model discount	$ 200.00	
5	Subtotal	=B3-B4	*cell reference*
6	Delivery	$ 59.00	

Result: The reference to cell B4 is entered into the formula.

13. Confirm the entry using the **enter key** ↵.

3.3.5   Calculating the billing amount

14. Select cell B7 and enter an equal sign (=) again.

5	Subtotal	$ 1,600.00
6	Delivery	$ 59.00
7	**Billing amount**	=
8		

15. Click on cell B5 to enter the reference of cell B5 into the formula.

4	Floor model discount	$ 200.00
5	Subtotal	$ 1,600.00
6	Delivery	$ 59.00
7	**Billing amount**	=**B5**
8		

mouse · *cell reference*

16. Enter a plus sign (+) using the keyboard.

4	Floor model discount	$ 200.00
5	Subtotal	$ 1,600.00
6	Delivery	$ 59.00
7	**Billing amount**	=**B5**+
8		

plus

17. Click on cell B6 to enter the cell reference of cell B6 into the formula.

4	Floor model discount	$ 200.00
5	Subtotal	$ 1,600.00
6	Delivery	$ 59.00
7	**Billing amount**	=**B5**+**B6**
8		

mouse · *cell reference*

18. Confirm the entry as usual using the **enter key** ⏎ .

3.3.6   Moving cells

The cells from A3 to B7 should be moved up by one row.

19. Select the cells from A3 to B7.

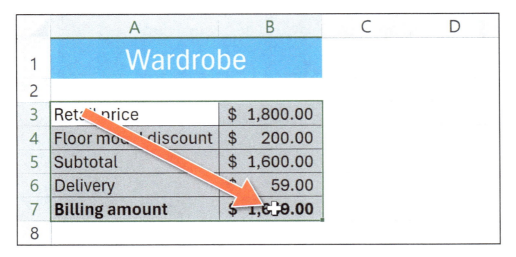

20. Point the mouse anywhere on the frame of the cell pointer. However, <u>do not</u> point to the fill handle.

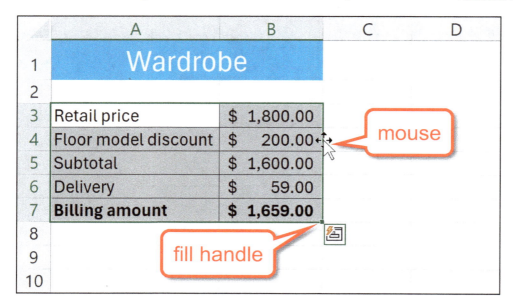

Result: The mouse pointer is displayed with a cross consisting of four arrows.

Advice: To move cells, the mouse must be placed on the edge of the selection. However, it <u>must</u> <u>not</u> be placed on the fill handle. This would activate the fill function.

21. Hold down the left mouse button and drag the mouse up by one line.

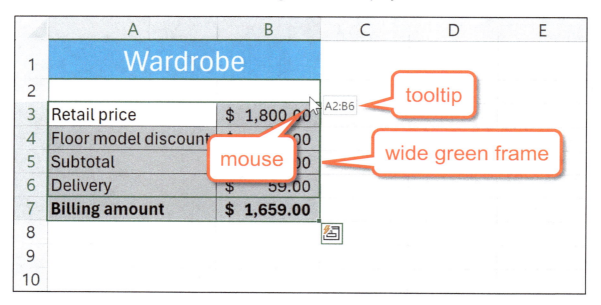

Advice: The wide green frame symbolizes the target area of the move. A **_tooltip_** with the new position of the selected area is also displayed.

22. Release the mouse button.

Result: The cells are moved. The cell references in the formulas are adjusted.

23. Undo the selection and look at the result.

	A	B	C	D
1	Wardrobe			
2	Retail price	$ 1,800.00		
3	Floor model discount	$ 200.00		
4	Subtotal	$ 1,600.00		
5	Delivery	$ 59.00		
6	**Billing amount**	**$ 1,659.00**		
7				

3.3.7 Checking the formulas

24. Select cell B4 and check the formula in the formula bar.

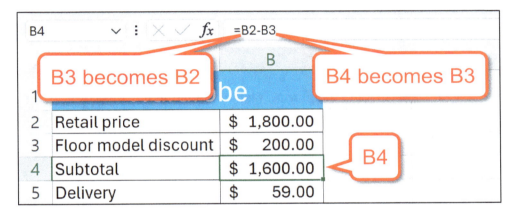

Advice: Moving the cells automatically adjusts the cell references

3.3.8 Saving

25. Complete the table with the figures shown.
    Advice: The changed zoom factor is saved in the file.

3.3.9 Checking the zoom factor

26. Open the file again to check the zoom factor setting.
    Result: The previously defined zoom factor of 130 % is still set when the file is reopened.
    Advice: New files are created with the default zoom factor of 100 %. Excel files are also referred to as workbooks.

3.3.10 Conclusion

27. Close Excel without saving again.

Repetitions

Repetitions are crucial when learning! We therefore recommend working through this book at least **twice** to consolidate your new knowledge.

4 Instruction: Temperatures

Use these instructions to create an evaluation of temperatures in different cities in the United States.

4.1 New content

- functions: MIN, MAX and AVERAGE
- decrease decimal
- middle align
- changing cell height
- repeating last action with F4
- copying multiple formulas at once

4.2 Repetitions

- SUM function

4.3 Instruction

4.3.1 Opening the sample file

1. Open the sample file **Chapter 04 - Temperatures - Start - B2**.
   Read more: The instructions for downloading the sample files can be found in chapter 2, page 3.

	A	B	C	D	E
1	Temperatures				
2	Highest values measured in Fahrenheit				
3					
4	City	Spring	Summer	Autumn	Winter
5	Anaheim	70	91	54	48
6	Chicago	66	97	57	48
7	Denver	72	97	57	52
8	Fresno	68	93	57	43
9	Houston	68	93	54	43
10	Las Vegas	72	100	52	54
11	Orlando	70	99	57	43
12	Sacramento	68	95	55	45
13	San Francisco	68	95	50	45
14	Vancouver	70	95	55	46
15	Washington D.C.	70	97	52	45
16	Worcester	72	99	54	52
17	Results				
18	Lowest temperature	66	91	50	43
19	Highest temperature	72	100	57	54
20	Average temperature	70	96	55	47
21					

Result: Temperatures

2. Click on the **Enable editing** button on the right side of the ribbon.

4.3.2 Determining the smallest number in an area

In the first part of the Excel introduction, you already became familiar with the SUM function. In addition to the SUM function, there are many other functions for different purposes. The MIN function is introduced below. It determines the smallest number in a range.

3. Enter the formula **=MIN(B5:B16)** into cell B18.

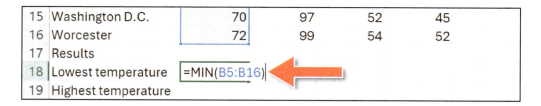

Advice: If the addition of these values had been the goal, the formula should be **=SUM(B5:B16)**. The only difference to the current input **=MIN(B5:B16)** is the function word **MIN**. You use the function word to give Excel a command. The command is: Calculate the smallest value from the following range. The range to be evaluated is specified in parentheses after the function word.

4. Confirm as usual by pressing the **enter key** ⏎ and look at the result.

Result: The smallest value in the specified range is the number 66.
Read more: Please also read Chapter 23 Explanation: Functions, page 142.

4.3.3   Determining the highest value

5. Enter the formula **=MAX(B5:B16)** in cell B19 to determine the largest value.

Advice: The **MAX** function is the counterpart to the MIN function. MAX determines the largest value from a range. The notation is identical to the SUM and MIN functions. Only the function word differs. The syntax of the MAX function is: **=MAX(range)**.

6. Look at the result.

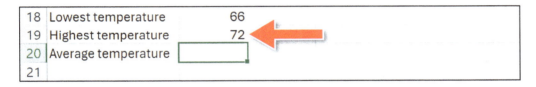

4.3.4   Calculating the average

You can use the AVERAGE function to calculate the average of several numbers. The structure of this function is identical to the previous functions SUM, MIN and MAX. The only difference is in the function word. The syntax is as follows: **=AVERAGE(range)**. The AVERAGE function adds and counts the values in the specified range. The result of the addition is then divided by the number of values.

7. Enter the formula **=AVERAGE(B5:B16)** in cell B20.

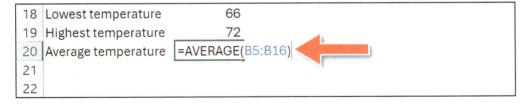

8. Look at the result. The average spring temperature is 69.5 °F.

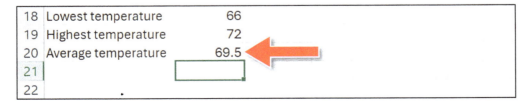

4.3.5   Consciously making mistakes

Mistakes cannot be avoided when learning. It is often useful to deliberately make a mistake in order to understand it better. Below you enter a formula in cell B21. It is mathematically correct but leads to a problem.

9. Enter the formula **=SUM(B5:B16)/12** in cell B21.

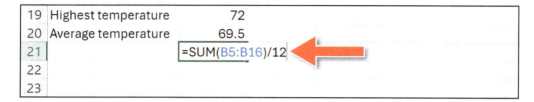

Advice: This formula is mathematically correct. It leads to the same result as the formula with the AVERAGE function in cell B20. The problem with this formula is the number 12. It was entered as a fixed value. If you were to delete numbers in the list and the number of values changed as a result, this formula would still divide the total by 12 (total = addition). The result would then be incorrect. For demonstration purposes, this error is then deliberately created.

10. Select the cells B5 to B7.

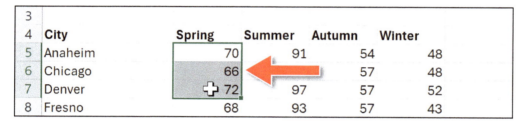

11. Press the **Delete key** [Delete] to delete the cells.
12. Look at the result.

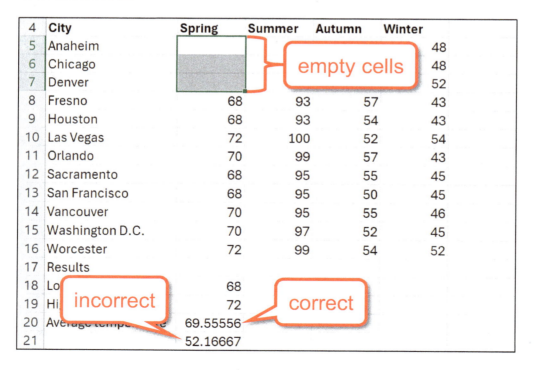

Advice: All currently visible spring temperatures are between 68 and 72 °F. The average must therefore lie between these values. The AVERAGE function in B20 displays the correct value. The sum of the numbers is divided by the actual number of values (9) is divided. B21 displays an incorrect value. The sum is still divided by 12 in B21. The AVERAGE function has another advantage. If you want to calculate the average of many numbers, AVERAGE counts the number of values faster and more reliably than a human being. Several cells can only be deleted at once with the **Delete key** ⬚Delete . the. This is not possible with the **backspace key** ⬚← in Excel.

13. Click twice on the **Undo** button ⬚↺ to restore the values in B5 to B7 and to remove the formula in B21.

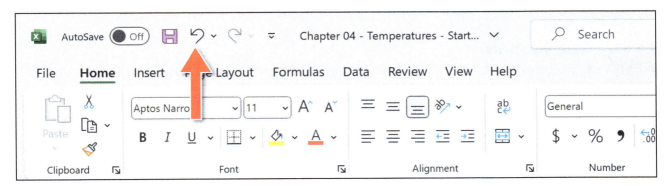

4.3.6   Decreasing decimal places

14. Select cell B20 and click on the **Decrease Decimal** button ⬚.00→.0 to hide a decimal place.

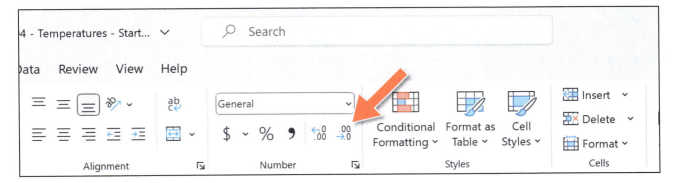

Result: The average temperature in B20 is displayed without decimal places.
Advice: Hidden decimal places are still considered when the cell is referenced in calculations. This will be shown in the example below.

4.3.7   Checking the hidden decimal place.

15. Enter the formula **=B20*2** in cell B21 to make the hidden decimal place apparent.

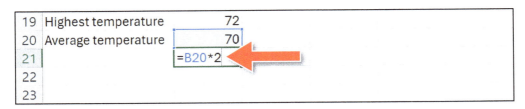

16. Confirm the entry using the **enter key** ⏎ and look at the result.

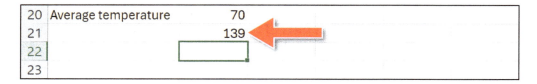

Result: The result 139 is displayed. It is the result of 69.5 * 2.

Advice: The displayed value 139 proves that the decimal places are still present. They are only hidden and are considered in all calculations.

17. Delete the calculation in cell B21 again. It was only used for demonstration purposes.

4.3.8 Copying formulas

In Part 1 of the Excel introduction, formulas were always copied individually. However, you can also copy several formulas at once.

18. Select the cells B18 to B20 and point to the fill handle with the mouse.

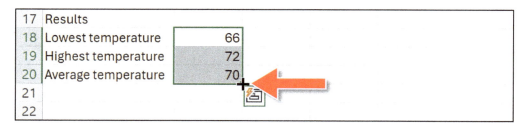

Result: The mouse pointer is displayed as a black cross ✚.

19. Drag the mouse to the right while holding down the left mouse button and copy the formula to columns C, D and E.

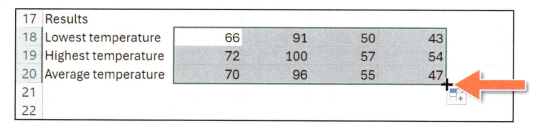

4.3.9 Selecting an entire row

20. Use the mouse to point to the row header of row 4.

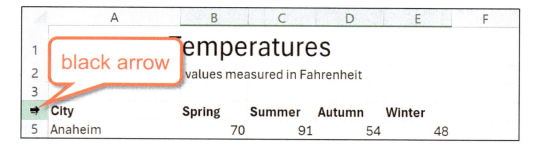

Result: The mouse pointer is displayed as a black arrow ➡.

21. Click on the row header of row 4 to select the entire row.

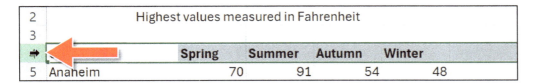

2	Highest values measured in Fahrenheit				
3					
➡		**Spring**	**Summer**	**Autumn**	**Winter**
5	Anaheim	70	91	54	48

    Advice: The black arrow ➡ is used to select an entire row.

22. Set the ***font size*** to ***12***.
    Result: All cells in row 4 are formatted with the font size 12. From column F onwards, the cells no longer contain any text. Changing the size has no visible effect there.
    Advice: Formatting an entire row is not useful for all formats. For example, it is less suitable for the ***fill color*** format. If you were to use this format, the empty cells from column F onwards would also be highlighted in color.

23. Select cells B4 to E4 and format the texts with ***Align Right*** ▤.

4.3.10   Changing the row height

24. Use the mouse to point to the dividing line between the row headers of rows 17 and 18.

16	Worc	72	99	54	52
17	Resu				
18	Lowe	66	91	50	43
19	Highest temperature	72	100	57	54

double arrow

    Result: The mouse is displayed as a double arrow ✛.

25. Hold down the left mouse button and drag the mouse downwards to increase the row height. Pay attention to the ***tooltip*** when dragging. The height should be approximately 60 pixels.

Height: 45.00 (60 pixels)   *tooltip*

16	Worcester		99	54	52
	Results				
	Lowest temperature		91	50	43
17	Highest temperature	72	100	57	54
18	Average temperature	70	96	55	47
19					

    Advice: The tooltip is a small help window.

26. Release the mouse button and look at the result.

16	Worcester	72	99	54	52
17	Results				
18	Lowest temperature	66	91	50	43

    Result: The text of A17 is displayed at the bottom of the cell.

4.3.11   Vertical text alignment

27. For cells A17 to E17, set the format ***Merge & Center*** ⊟.

28. Click on the **Middle Align** button ☰ to center the text vertically.

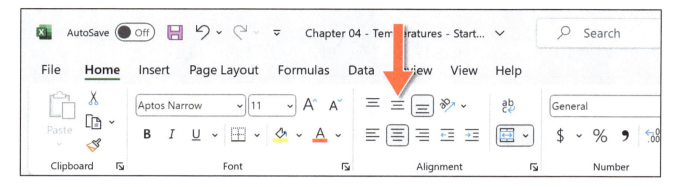

29. Format cell A7 with **bold** and **font size 12**. Look at the result.

16	Worcester	72	99	54	52
17	**Results**				
18	Lowest temperature	66	91	50	43

4.3.12   Creating a color change

30. Select the cells A5 to E5. Press and hold the **control key** ⌷Ctrl. Then select cells A7 to E7.

4	**City**	**Spring**	**Summer**	**Autumn**	**Winter**
5	Anaheim	70	91	54	48
6	Chicago	66	97	57	48
7	Denver	72	97	57	52
8	Fresno	68	93	57	43

   Result: Holding down the control key retains the first selection.

31. Keep the **control key** ⌷Ctrl pressed and select every second line.
32. Select lines 18 and 20 as well.
33. Set the fill color to **Orange, Accent 2, Lighter 60%**.

4.3.13   Formatting borders

34. Select the cells A5 to E16.

35. Click on the arrow ⌄ next to the **borders** button ⊞⌄ to open the list box for this button.

36. Click on the list item **More borders** ⊞.

   ◇ Erase Border

   🖊 Line Color   >

   Line Style   >

   ⊞ More Borders...

Result: The *Format Cells* dialog box is displayed.

37. Click on the *Outside* button 🔲 and on the button for the vertical dividing line 🔳. The horizontal dividing lines should not be set.

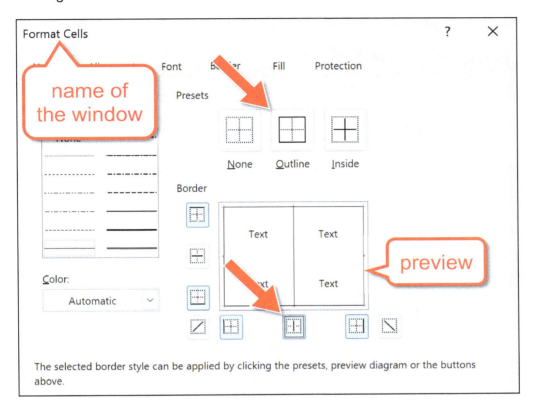

Result: The preview shows the currently set borders.

38. Click on the *OK* button, undo to selection and look at the result.

4	City	Spring	Summer	Autumn	Winter
5	Anaheim	70	91	54	48
6	Chicago	66	97	57	48
7	D	72	97	57	52
8	F	68	93	57	43
9	H	68	93	54	43
10	L	72	100	52	54
11	Orlando	70	99	57	43
12	Sacramento	68			45
13	San Francisco	68			45
14	Vancouver	70			46
15	Washington D.C.	70	97	52	45
16	Worcester	72	99	54	52

Result: The border is assigned to the selected area.

4.3.14   Reassign border

39. Select the cells A18 to E20.

40. Press the **function key** $\boxed{F4}$ to repeat the last operation.

    Attention: If you are working on a laptop, you sometimes have to use the key combination **Fn key** $\boxed{Fn}$ + $\boxed{F4}$ to activate $\boxed{F4}$. Also make sure that you do not perform any further steps between assigning the border and pressing the F4 key. F4 would not work in this case.

    Advice: The **Fn** key is only available on laptops and smaller keyboards. The abbreviation **Fn** stands for function.

41. Undo the selection and look at the result.

	City	Spring	Summer	Autumn	Winter
3					
4	City	Spring	Summer	Autumn	Winter
5	Anaheim	70	91	54	48
6	Chicago	66	97	57	48
7	Denver	72	97	57	52
8	Fresno	68	93	57	43
9	Houston	68	93	54	43
10	Las Vegas	72	100	52	54
11	Orlando	70	99	57	43
12	Sacramento	68	95	55	45
13	San Francisco	68	95	50	45
14	Vancouver	70	95	55	46
15	Washington D.C.	70	97	52	45
16	Worcester	72	9		
	Results			copied border	
17					
18	Lowest temperature	66	91	50	43
19	Highest temperature	72	100	57	54
20	Average temperature	70	96	55	47
21					

Result: The previously set borders are reassigned.

Advice: Pressing the **function key** $\boxed{F4}$ repeats the last step.

42. Save the file and close Excel.

Do you need help?

Do you have any questions about this book or Excel? Write us an email and we will be happy to help you personally! Please also look at our homepage on the Internet. We have prepared some help topics for you there.

Email: info@ityco.com

Internet: www.ityco.com → Help

5   Instruction: Clothing

Use these instructions to evaluate the sales figures of clothing items.

5.1   New content

- error checking
- Auto Fill Options
- selecting areas in formulas with the mouse (pointing method)
- thousands separator

5.2   Repetitions

- functions: SUM, MIN, MAX, AVERAGE
- moving cells

	A	B	C	D	E	F	G	H	I
1				**Clothing**					
2				Pieces sold per year					
3									
4	**Item**	**2021**	**2022**	**2023**		**Minimum**	**Maximum**	**Average**	**Sum**
5	Jeans	152,413	168,452	178,452		152,413	178,452	166,439	499,317
6	Skirts	104,523	106,397	129,710		104,523	129,710	113,543	340,630
7	Dresses	139,703	142,987	150,365		139,703	150,365	144,352	433,055
8	Tops	80,301	82,104	89,622		80,301	89,622	84,009	252,027
9	Coats	40,366	41,787	43,019		40,366	43,019	41,724	125,172
10									
11									
12	Minimum	40,366	41,787	43,019					
13	Maximum	152,413	168,452	178,452					
14	Average	103,461	108,345	118,234					
15	Sum	517,306	541,727	591,168					
16									

Result: Clothing

5.3   Instruction

5.3.1   Opening the sample file

1. Open the sample file **Chapter 05 - Clothing - Start - B2** and enable editing.
    Read more: The instructions for downloading the sample files can be found in chapter 2, page 3.

5.3.2   Determining the lowest value

2. Enter the formula **=MIN(B5:D5)** in cell F5 to determine the smallest value.

Result: In order to quickly identify the selected area, it is highlighted in color. The selected area is displayed in blue inside the parentheses. The corresponding cells area framed in the same color.

5.3.3   Determining the highest value

3. Enter the formula **=MAX(B5:D5)** in cell G5 to determine the largest value.

5.3.4   Determining the average value

4.   Enter the formula **=AVERAGE(B5:D5)** in H5 to calculate the average.

2023		Minimum	Maximum	Average	Sum
178452		152413	178452	=AVERAGE(B5:D5)	
129710					

Advice: The AVERAGE function performs three calculation steps. First, the numbers in the specified range are added together. Then the number of numbers in this range is counted. In the third step, the sum of the values is divided by the number of numbers to determine the average. You can always enter function names and cell references in lower case. Upper case is the standard spelling for functions and cell references. Excel therefore automatically converts lower-case letters to upper-case letters at the end of the input. The syntax **=average(b5:d5)** becomes **=AVERAGE(B5:D5)**.

5.   Determine the sum of the cells from B5 to D5 in cell I5 (i5).

2023		Minimum	Maximum	Average	Sum
178452		152413	178452	166439	=SUM(B5:D5)
129710					

5.3.5   Copying formulas

6.   Select the cells F5 to I5 (i5). Point to the fill handle with the mouse.

2023		Minimum	Maximum	Average	Sum
178452		152413	178452	166439	499317
129710					
150365					

Result: The mouse pointer is displayed as a black cross **+**.

7.   Hold the left mouse button and drag the mouse to row 9 to copy the formulas to the cells below.

5.3.6   Auto Fill Options

8.   Undo the selection and look at the result.

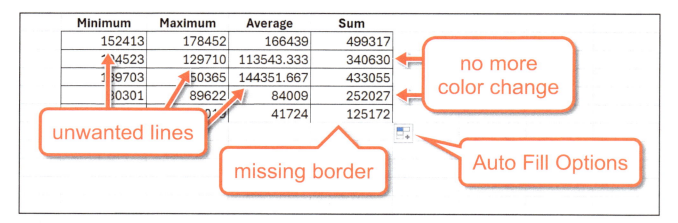

Result: The formulas are copied. The formats of row 5 are also copied at the same time. They overwrite the previous borders and the color change. The **Auto Fill Options** button appears at the bottom right of the selected area.

Advice: When filling cells, the contents <u>and</u> formats are copied by default.

9. Click on the **Auto Fill Options** button ⊞ to open the list box for this button.

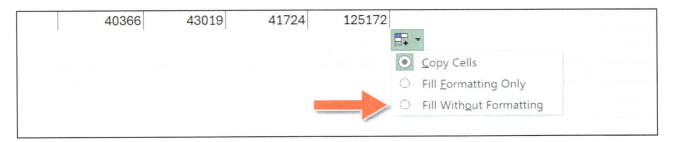

10. Click on the Fill without formatting list item inside the list box to restore the previous formatting.

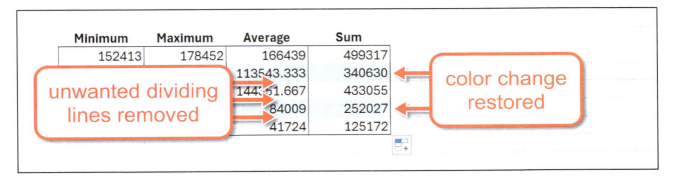

11. Undo the selection and look at the result.

Minimum	Maximum	Average	Sum
152413	178452	166439	499317
		113543.333	340630
		144351.667	433055
		84009	252027
		41724	125172

> unwanted dividing lines removed

> color change restored

Result: The previous formats are restored.

5.3.7   Error checking

Excel automatically checks tables for possible errors and highlights them with a green triangle. However, Excel cannot detect all errors beyond doubt. Sometimes even correct calculations are marked as errors. The following example will familiarize you with these situations.

12. Enter the formula **=MIN(B5:B9)** in cell B11 to determine the smallest value.

	Item	2021	2022	2023		Minimum	Maximum	Average
4	Item	2021	2022	2023		Minimum	Maximum	Average
5	Jeans	152413	168452	178452		152413	178452	166439
6	Skirts	104523	106397	129710		104523	129710	113543.333
7	Dresses	139703	142987	150365		139703	150365	144351.667
8	Tops	80301	82104	89622		80301	89622	84009
9	Coats	40366	41787	43019		40366	43019	41724
10								
11	Minimum	=MIN(B5:B9)						
12	Maximum							

13. Complete the entry as usual and look at the result.

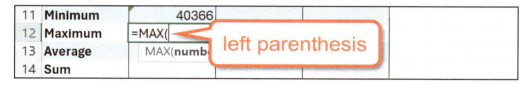

4	Item	2021	2022	2023	Minimum	Maximum	Average
5	Jeans	152413				178452	166439
6	Skirts	104523	106			129710	113543.333
7	Dresse		142987	150365	139703	150365	144351.667
8	Tops		82104	89622	80301	89622	84009
9	Coats		41787	43019	40366	43019	41724
10							
11	Minimum	40366					
12	Maximum						
13	Average						

(callouts: "B4 contains a number", "green triangle")

Result: The result is displayed. A green triangle also appears at the top left of cell B11.
Advice: Excel <u>suspects</u> an error in this calculation. The green triangle indicates this. However, the formula is correct! B4 contains a number and is directly adjacent to the range B5 to B9. Excel therefore believes that B4 was forgotten during input and points this out to you. Excel does not recognize that this year is a heading. Ignore the green triangle in this situation.

5.3.8   Selecting an area using the pointing method

Up to now, you have always entered the range in a function (SUM, MIN, MAX or AVERAGE) by hand. However, the cell range can also be selected with the mouse. This simplifies input and reduces typing errors. This procedure is also known as the pointing method.

14. Enter the partial formula **=MAX(** in B12. However, do not complete the entry yet.

11	Minimum	40366
12	Maximum	=MAX(
13	Average	MAX(numb
14	Sum	

(callout: "left parenthesis")

Attention: Enter the partial formula exactly up to the left parenthesis (round opening bracket).
Advice: The formula is not complete yet. The area to be evaluated is then selected with the mouse.

15. Click on cell B5 and while holding down the left mouse button drag the mouse to cell B9 to copy this range to the formula.

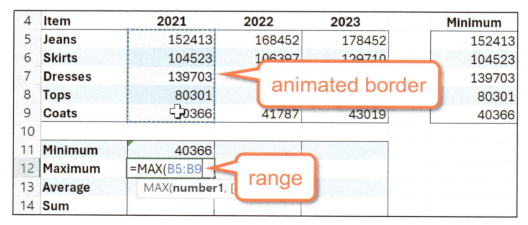

4	Item	2021	2022	2023	Minimum
5	Jeans	152413	168452	178452	152413
6	Skirts	104523	106397	129710	104523
7	Dresses	139703			139703
8	Tops	80301			80301
9	Coats	0366	41787	43019	40366
10					
11	Minimum	40366			
12	Maximum	=MAX(B5:B9			
13	Average	MAX(**number1**, [			
14	Sum				

(callouts: "animated border", "range")

Result: The selected area is highlighted with an animated border and is copied to the formula.

16. Press the **enter key** ↵ to complete the entry.

11	Minimum	40366
12	Maximum	152413
13	Average	
14	Sum	

Result: The result is displayed. A green triangle also appears in cell B12.
Advice: The right parenthesis (round closing bracket) is an integral part of all functions. It therefore does not need to be entered in many situations. Excel adds the parenthesis automatically.

17. Select cell B12 and check whether the right parenthesis is present.

Result: The right parenthesis was automatically added when the entry was completed.

5.3.9   Determining the average using the pointing method

18. Enter the partial formula **=AVERAGE(** in B13. However, do not complete the entry yet.

12	Maximum	152413
13	Average	=AVERAGE(
14	Sum	AVERAGE(numbe
15		

left parenthesis

19. Click on cell B5 and while holding down the left mouse button drag the mouse to cell B9 to copy this range to the formula.

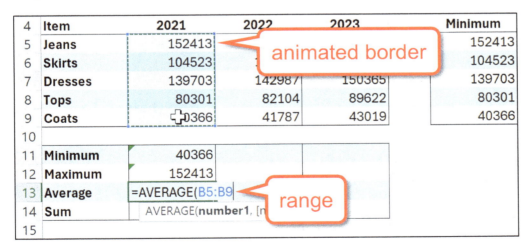

Result: The selected area is highlighted with an animated border and is copied to the formula.

20. Complete the entry.
Advice: The right parenthesis is usually added automatically when you confirm the input. However, there are also situations in which the automatic correction concerning the right parenthesis does not work as smoothly as it does here.

5.3.10   Determining the total

21. Determine the sum for the range B5 to B9 in cell B14. Use the pointing method again.

5.3.11   Copying formulas

22. Select the range B11 to B14 and copy the formulas up to column D.

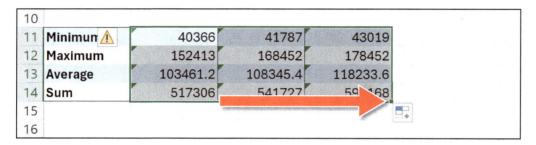

> **Advice:** As the formulas are copied horizontally, the color change is retained.

5.3.12   Thousands separator

To make the numbers easier to read, they should be formatted with a thousands separator (,). The thousands separator is a comma and belongs to the **number formats**.

23. Use the **control key** Ctrl to create multiple selections at once. Select the areas B5 to D9, F5 to I9 (i9) and B11 to D14.

24. Click on the small arrow ⬏ at the bottom right of the **Number** group to open the **Format Cells** dialog box.

> **Advice:** The **Format Cells** dialog box is one of the most important dialog boxes in Excel. Almost all formats for cells can be switched on and off here. There are different ways to open this dialog box.

25. Click on the **Number** category in the **Number** tab to activate it.

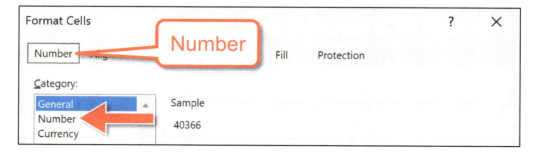

> **Advice:** The **Number** tab contains all formats that can be set for numbers.

26. Make the following changes:
    • Decimal places: 0
    • Use 1000 Separator: Enable (check the box)

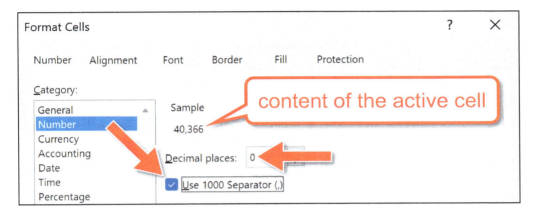

Result: The example shows the result of the settings. The displayed number 40,366 is the content of the active cell (B11). A comma (,) is displayed as the thousands separator. It is placed after every third digit from the right to improve the legibility of the number. Millions and billions are also easier for the eye to recognize in this way.

27. Click on the **OK** button to apply the changes.
28. Undo the selection and look at the result.

Item	2021	2022	2023		Minimum	Maximum	Average	Sum
Jeans	152,413	168,452	178,452		152,413	178,452	166,439	499,317
Skirts	104,523	106,397	129,710		104,523	129,710	113,543	340,630
Dresses	139,703	142,987	150,365		139,703	150,365	144,352	433,055
Tops	80,301	82,104	89,622		80,301	89,622	84,009	252,027
Coats	40,366	41,787	43,019		40,366	43,019	41,724	125,172
Minimum	40,366	41,787	43,019					
Maximum	152,413	168,452	178,452					
Average	103,461	108,345	118,234					
Sum	517,306	541,727	591,168					

5.3.13   Moving cells

Cells A11 to D14 should be lowered by one cell.

29. Select the cells A11 to D14.

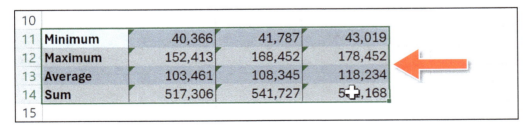

30. Point the mouse anywhere on the edge of the selection. However, do <u>not</u> point to the fill handle.

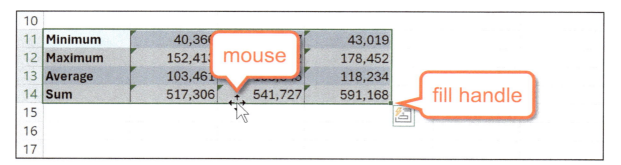

Result: The mouse pointer is displayed with a cross consisting of four arrows ⤡.
Advice: This mouse pointer symbolizes the moving of cells.

31. Hold down the left mouse button and drag the mouse down one row. Pay attention to the wide green frame.

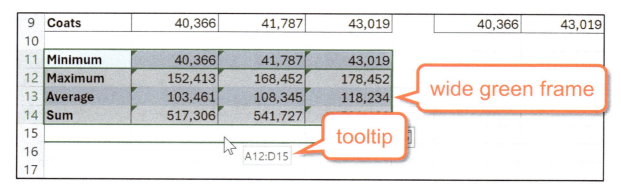

Result: The wide green frame shows the new position of the area. A ***tooltip*** is displayed next to the mouse pointer. The tooltip shows the new position as the range A12 to D15.

5.3.14   Conclusion

32. Click on ***Save*** 💾 to save the workbook.

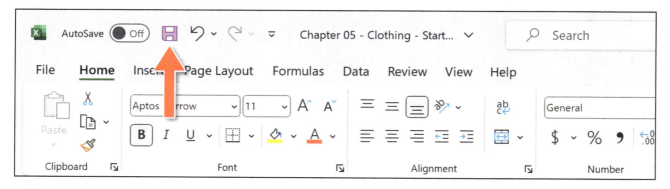

33. Close Excel.

6   Instruction: Butchery

Use these instructions to calculate the profit for several butcher's stores.

6.1   New content

- widening several columns
- inserting columns
- single cell minus sum of an area
- adjusting column width to a specific word
- summing up two areas

	A	B	C	D	E	F	G
1				Butchery			
2							
3	**Branch**	**New York**	**Austin**	**Detroit**	**Houston**	**Sum**	**Average**
4	Revenue	$ 1,502,145.00	$ 1,024,587.00	$ 1,289,574.00	$ 1,865,412.00	$ 5,681,718.00	$ 1,420,429.50
5							
6				Costs			
7	Goods	$ 360,514.80	$ 245,900.88	$ 315,648.25	$ 447,698.88	$ 1,369,762.81	$ 342,440.70
8	Wages	$ 460,686.40	$ 321,867.84	$ 399,852.61	$ 546,931.84	$ 1,729,338.69	$ 432,334.67
9	Rent	$ 140,214.50	$ 104,458.70	$ 121,692.00	$ 166,541.20	$ 532,906.40	$ 133,226.60
10	Electricity	$ 15,021.45	$ 10,245.87	$ 13,208.25	$ 18,654.12	$ 57,129.69	$ 14,282.42
11	Insurances	$ 14,230.54	$ 9,801.00	$ 12,198.59	$ 18,097.23	$ 54,327.36	$ 13,581.84
12	Heating	$ 30,042.90	$ 20,491.74	$ 25,289.33	$ 37,308.24	$ 113,132.21	$ 28,283.05
13	**Profit**	$ 481,434.41	$ 311,820.97	$ 401,684.97	$ 630,180.49	$ 1,825,120.84	
14							
15							
16							
17	Energy costs	$ 170,261.90					
18							

Result: Butchery

6.2   Repetitions

- numbers that have been made unrecognizable by number signs (#)
- opening edit mode with F2
- copying formulas

6.3   Instructions

6.3.1   *Opening the sample file*

1. Open the sample file ***Chapter 06 - Butchery - Start - B2*** and enable editing.
2. Look at the table.

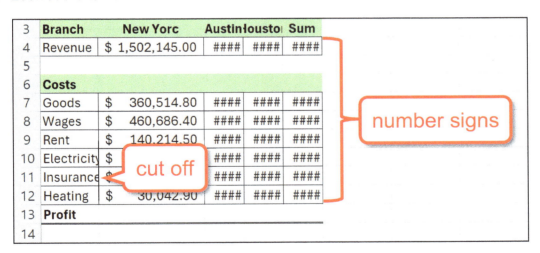

Result: In some cells, number signs (#) are displayed instead of numbers. The words ***Electricity*** and ***Insurances*** in cells A10 and A11 are cut off.

Advice: If a word is too long for a column and the neighboring cell is filled, this word is cut off. Excel behaves differently with numbers. Numbers are <u>never</u> truncated. If a number is too long for a column, the number is made unrecognizable by number signs (#). The number signs are therefore a protective function. In this way, Excel prevents the display and printing of incorrect numbers. Number signs are often also referred to as ***hashes***, ***pound signs*** or ***hashtags***. However, the term hashtag is not used in Excel. It usually refers to social networks such as Twitter or Instagram.

6.3.2   Checking cell content

3. Select cell C4 to read the content of the cell in the formula bar.

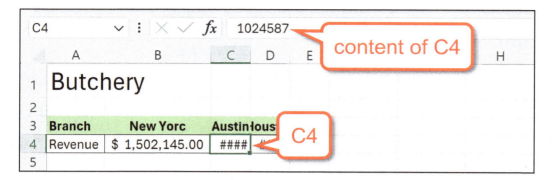

Advice: Even if numbers have been obscured by number signs, they can still be read inside the formula bar.

6.3.3   Adjusting the width of several columns simultaneously

4. Click on the column header of column an drag the mouse to the column header of column E to select these three columns.

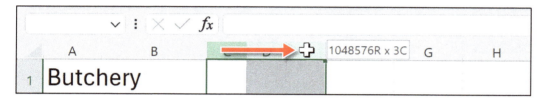

5. Click on the **Format** button [Format ∨] to open the list box.

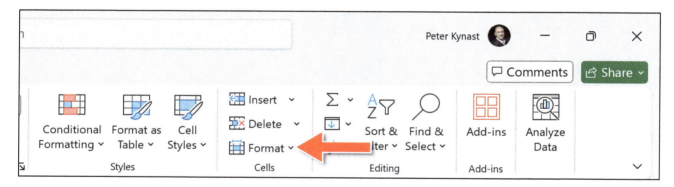

Advice: Depending on the size of your screen, the display of the buttons may vary. The button is displayed larger on larger monitors (see the following illustration).

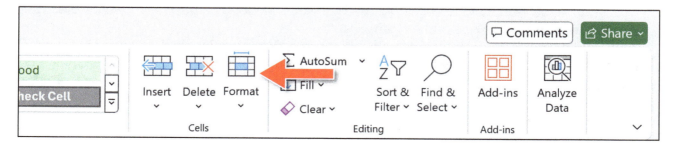

6. Click on **AutoFit Column Width** in the list box.

> **Result:** The column width is increased. The width depends on the longest content in each column. The number signs disappear and all numbers are visible now.

6.3.4   Correcting content

Corrections can be made via the formula bar or directly in the cell. Both methods are equivalent. However, editing directly in the cell is easier in many cases.

7. Select cell B3. Press the **function key** $\boxed{F2}$ to activate edit mode.

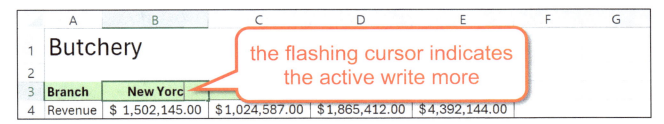

> **Advice:** The F in $\boxed{F2}$ stands for function key. The function keys have different functions depending on the program.
> **Attention:** If you are currently working on a laptop or with a smaller keyboard, you sometimes have to use the key combination **Fn key** $\boxed{Fn}$ + $\boxed{F2}$ to activate $\boxed{F2}$. The Fn key is only available on laptops or small keyboard.
> **Read more:** Please also read Chapter 26 Explanation: Keyboard shortcuts, page 146.

8. Delete the letter **c** and enter a **k**.
9. Complete the entry as usual by pressing the **enter key** $\boxed{\hookleftarrow}$.

3	Branch	New York	Austin	Houston	Sum
4	Revenue	$ 1,502,145.00	$1,024,587.00	$1,865,412.00	$4,392,144.00
5					

6.3.5   Inserting columns

A new column for the city of **Detroit** is to be inserted between columns C and D. As the new column is inserted between the existing cities, the sum function in cell E4 is automatically adjusted. To check, first look at the formula in E4.

10. Select cell E4 and check the formula for this cell in the formula bar. It reads **=SUM(B4:D4)**.
11. Click on any cell in column D to Select this column.

Advice: It is also possible to select the entire column D.

12. Click on the arrow ⌄ next to the **Insert** button 📋 Insert ⌄ to open the list box for this button.

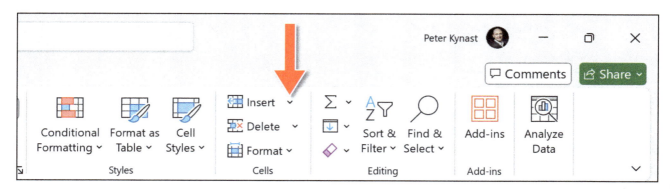

Advice: The display of the buttons may vary depending on the size of your screen. On larger monitors, the **Insert** button is displayed larger (see illustration below). In this case, the arrow is located below the button.

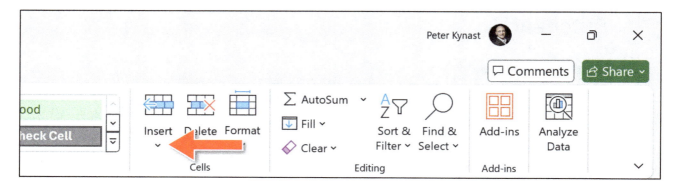

13. Click on the **Insert Sheet Columns** list item in the list box of this button.

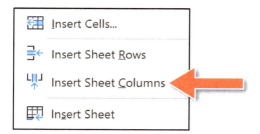

Result: A new column is inserted to the left of column D. It adopts the formats of the adjacent columns. The formulas in the sum column F are adjusted.

Advice: New columns are always inserted to the left of the selected column. You can also insert columns <u>before</u> column A in this way. New rows are always inserted <u>above</u> the selected row. You can therefore also insert new rows above row 1.

6.3.6   Checking the formula

14. Select cell F4 and look at the formula **=SUM(B4:E4)** in this cell.

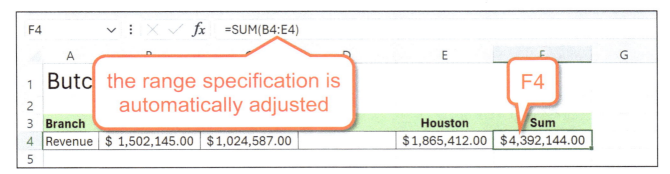

Result: The range specification was automatically adjusted.

Attention: In many cases, Excel automatically corrects the cell references. However, these automatic changes do not always work as you might expect. Various examples of this will be shown in future books. Always carry out checks as long as you are not yet familiar with automatic formatting.

15. Enter the following data for the city of **Detroit** in the empty column. However, do not enter the commas when entering the data.

3	Branch	New York	Austin	Detroit	Houston	Sum
4	Revenue	$ 1,502,145.00	$1,024,587.00	$1,289,574.00	$1,865,412.00	$5,681,718.00
5						
6	Costs					
7	Goods	$ 360,514.80	$ 245,900.88	$ 315,648.25	$ 4...	
8	Wages	$ 460,686.40	$ 321,867.84	$ 399,852.61	$ 5...	data for Detroit
9	Rent	$ 140,214.50	$ 104,458.70	$ 121,692.00	$ 1...	
10	Electricity	$ 15,021.45	$ 10,245.87	$ 13,208.25	$ 18,654.12	$ 57,129.69
11	Insurance	$ 14,230.54	$ 9,801.00	$ 12,198.59	$ 18,097.23	$ 54,327.36
12	Heating	$ 30,042.90	$ 20,491.74	$ 25,289.33	$ 37,308.24	$ 113,132.21

Advice: The commas (thousands separators) are displayed automatically due to the dollar format. This happens when you confirm the entry. The decimal point (.) however must be typed manually.

6.3.7   Automatic continuation of the formatting

16. Enter the heading **Average** in cell G3.

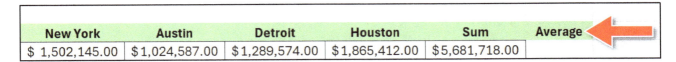

Result: When confirming the entry, cell G3 automatically adopts the formats (fill color and centering) of the adjacent cells on the left.

Advice: The following applies to many formats: If a format has been used at least three times without interruption, the formatting is automatically continued when filling an adjacent cell. However, there are also formats that are not automatically continued.

6.3.8   Determining the average

17. In cell G4, determine the average of cells B4 to E4 using the pointing method (mouse selection).

18. Look at the result.

Austin	Detroit	Houston	Sum	Average
$1,024,587.00	$1,289,574.00	$1,865,412.00	$5,681,718.00	$1,420,429.50

Result: As the result is wider than the column, the width is automatically adjusted. The **_border_** format is not automatically continued in this situation.

19. Format cell G4 with **_All Borders_** ⊞.

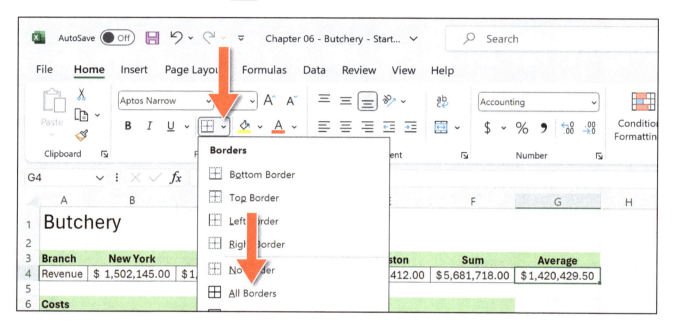

6.3.9   *Copying the formula*

The formula in G4 is to be copied to cells G7 to G12. Copying with the fill handle is possible. However, it has the disadvantage that cells G5 and G6 are also filled in. The contents and formats of these cells would then have to be deleted again. To avoid this the formula in G4 is copied to the cells from G7 to G12. The cell references are automatically adjusted in the same way as when copying with the fill handle.

20. Select cell G4 and click on the **_Copy_** button 📋 to copy the formula of cell G4. Do <u>not</u> click on the arrow ⌄ next to the button.

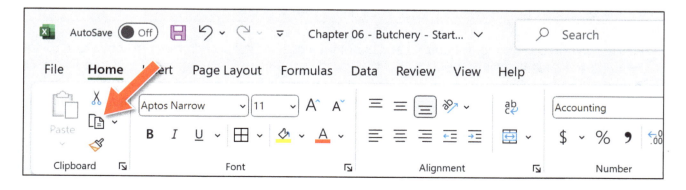

Result: The formula is copied. The animated frame symbolizes the active copy mode.

Advice: Depending on the size of your screen, the display of the buttons may vary. On larger monitors, the **Copy** larger button (see illustration below) is displayed. In this case, click on the symbol or the word of the button.

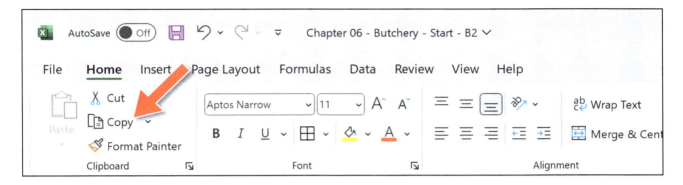

21. Select cells G7 to G12.

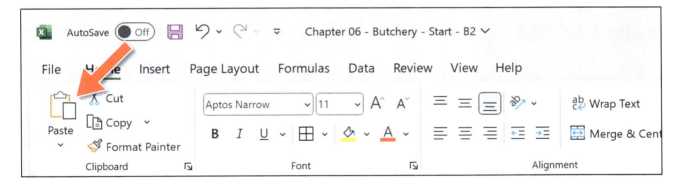

Detroit	Houston	Sum	Average
$1,289,574.00	$1,865,412.00	$5,681,718.00	$1,420,429.50
$ 315,648.25	$ 447,698.88	$1,369,762.81	
$ 399,852.61	$ 546,931.84	$1,729,338.69	
$ 121,692.00	$ 166,541.20	$ 532,906.40	
$ 13,208.25	$ 18,654.12	$ 57,129.69	
$ 12,198.59	$ 18,097.23	$ 54,327.36	
$ 25,289.33	$ 37,308.24	$ 113,132.21	

target area

Advice: G7 to G12 is the target range. The formula should be inserted here.

22. Click on the **Paste** button to insert the formula into the selected cells.

Attention: Do not click on the word **Paste** or on the arrow below the button.

Result: The cell references are automatically adjusted when pasting.

Advice: When copying formulas, Excel behaves in the same way as when filling cells with the black cross. If a formula is copied to a cell that is below the original cell, the numbers of the cell references (row entries) are adjusted. If a formula is copied to horizontally, the letters (column entries) are changed.

23. Look at the result.

Detroit	Houston	Sum	Average
$1,289,574.00	$1,865,412.00	$5,681,718.00	$1,420,429.50
$ 315,648.25	$ 447,698.88	$1,369,762.81	$ 342,440.70
$ 399,852.61	$ 546,931.84	$1,729,338.69	$ 432,334.67
$ 121,692.00	$ 166,541.20	$ 532,906.40	$ 133,226.60
$ 13,208.25	$ 18,654.12	$ 57,129.69	$ 14,282.42
$ 12,198.59	$ 18,097.23	$ 54,327.36	$ 13,581.84
$ 25,289.33	$ 37,308.24	$ 113,132.21	$ 28,283.05

animated border

results

🗐 (Ctrl) ▾

Result: When copying, the dollar format and the border formatting are also copied.

Advice: Copy mode is active as long as the animated border is visible. The copied content could be pasted into other cells. This mode can be terminated with the **Escape key** Esc. However, it would also be terminated automatically the next time content is entered into a cell.

6.3.10   *Single cell minus the sum of several numbers*

Excel 365 - Part 1 contains the instructions for a housekeeping budget. The housekeeping budget has a similar task to the butchery instruction. Several costs are to be offset against the income. In the budget calculation, the costs are first added up in a separate cell. Then the costs are deducted from the wages in another cell. In the butchery instruction, the profit is calculated without first adding the costs. The entire calculation takes place in <u>one</u> cell.

24. Enter the formula **=B4-SUM(B7:B12)** in cell B13 to determine the profit.

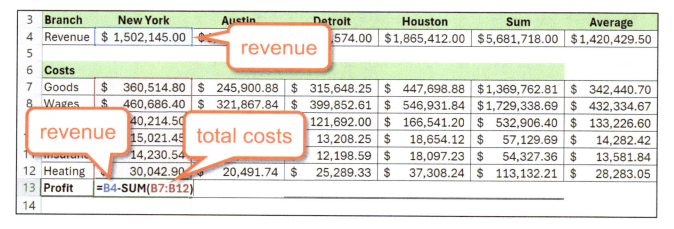

Advice: B4 is the revenue. The total costs are deducted from this revenue. In most cases, you can omit the right parenthesis. Excel automatically adds them without asking. In this situation, the right parenthesis must be entered. A correction for the formula is be suggested when confirming the entry.

25. Copy the formula to the adjacent cells C13 to F13.

Advice: In this situation, it makes no difference whether you use the black cross ✚ or copy the formula into the target area.

6.3.11   Adjusting the column width to a specific word

The heading **butchery** is the widest cell in column A. If you double-click on the separator between the column headers A and B, the column width would adapt to this word. The second longest entry in column A is **Energy costs** in A17. The width of A should be adapted to this cell.

26. Select cell A17 and click on the **Format** button.

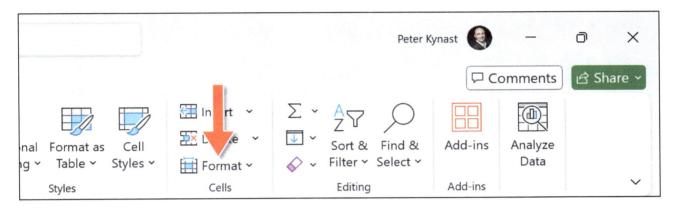

27. Click on **AutoFit Column Width** to adjust the column width to the cell content **Energy costs**.

6.3.12   Functions with two areas

The energy costs for electricity and gas are to be determining in B17. The corresponding values can be found in the ranges B10 to E10 and B12 to E12.

28. Enter the formula **=SUM(B10:E10,B12:E12)** in cell B17 to add the costs for electricity and heating. Pay attention to the comma between the ranges.

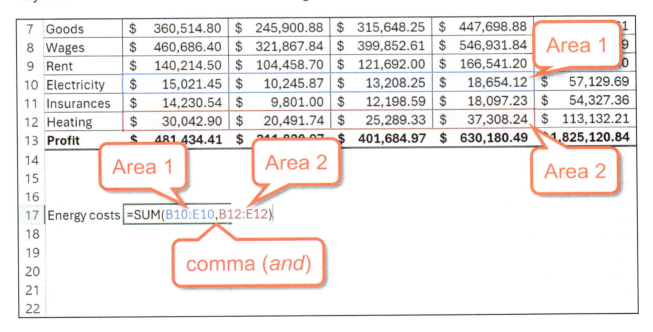

Advice: Previously, the functions always had only one range in parentheses. This sum function contains two ranges. They are separated by a comma (,). A colon (:) in the range specification means **to**. The comma (,) means **and**. The formula therefore reads as follows: Form the sum of the ranges B10 to E10 and B12 to E12. This way of writing can also be transferred to other functions, e.g. MIN, MAX or AVERAGE. More than two ranges are also possible. You get the same result with the notation **=SUM(B10:E10)+SUM(B12:E12)**, but shorter notations should be preferred.

6.3.13 Formatting

29. Click on the row header of row 3 to select this row.

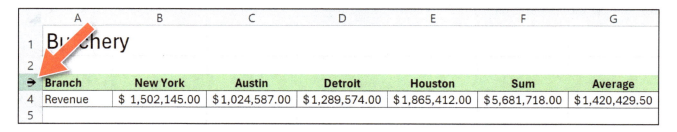

Advice: When you click on the row header, the mouse is displayed as a black arrow ➡.

30. Format the row in **font size 12**.

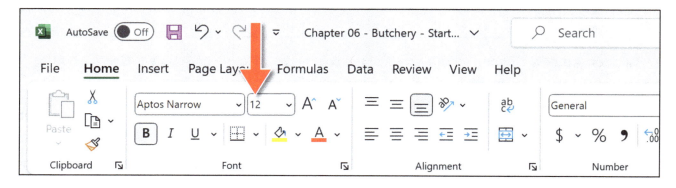

31. Merge and center the Cells A1 to G1 and A6 to G6.

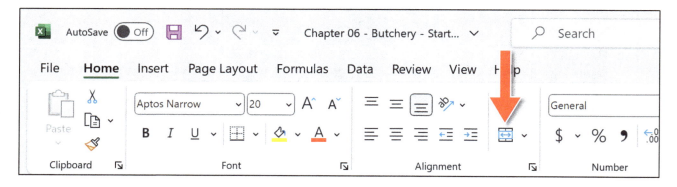

6.3.14 Conclusion

32. Save the file and close Excel.

7   Instruction: Data usage

Use these instructions to evaluate the monthly internet data volume of a family over the last two years in order to calculate a new cell phone contract.

7.1   New content

- format painter
- moving cells between other cells
- manual line breaks in cells
- average value of two ranges
- AutoSum

		Sum 2022 + 2023	Average per month
19	Mom	15.0	0.6
20	Dad	22.0	0.9
21	Helen	54.3	2.3
22	Max	44.5	1.9
23	Alexander	45.1	1.9
24		180.8	7.5

Result: Data usage

7.2   Repetitions

- decrease decimal
- sum of two areas
- copying formulas automatically by double-clicking
- functions: SUM, AVERAGE

7.3   Instruction

7.3.1   Opening the sample file

1. Open the sample file **Chapter 07 - Data usage - Start - B2** and enable editing.

7.3.2   Decreasing decimal places

The data usage should be displayed with one decimal place.

2. Select the range from B5 to M9. Click on the **Decrease Decimal** button to hide a decimal place for the selected numbers.

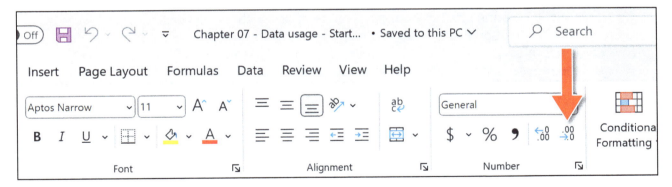

Advice: The decimal places are only hidden. All digits are considered when calculating.

3. Click on the **Decrease Decimal** button again to hide the second decimal place as well.

7.3.3   Copying formats

The table for 2023 should have the same format as the table for 2022.

4. Click on any cell in the range from A4 to M9.
5. Use the keyboard shortcut **control key** Ctrl + A to select the whole table.
   Advice: Excel uses this keyboard shortcut to select cells that are recognized as a connected table.
6. Click on the **Format Painter** button 🖌 to copy the format of this area.

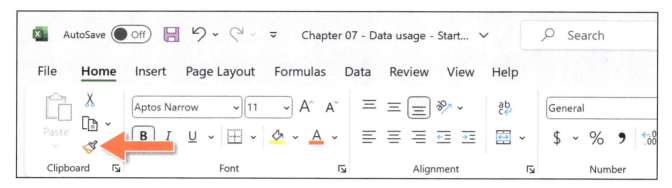

Result: The formats of this area are copied. The content is not copied. The selected area is highlighted by an animated frame.
7. Point to cell A11 with the mouse. First look at the following illustration. Do not click on cell A11 yet.

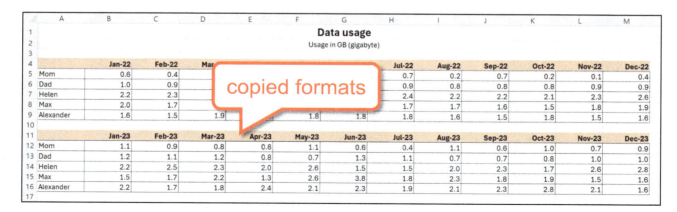

Result: A brush 🖌 is displayed next to the white cross ⊕. The brush symbolizes the active **Format Painter** tool.
Advice: Pointing means placing the mouse on a position without clicking.
8. Click on cell A11 to copy the formats to the range from A11 onwards.
   Result: The formats of the A4 to M9 selection are copied to the range from A11 to M16.
9. Release the mouse button and look at the result.

	A	B	C	D	E	F	G	H	I	J	K	L	M
1							Data usage						
2							Usage in GB (gigabyte)						
3													
4		Jan-22	Feb-22	Mar				Jul-22	Aug-22	Sep-22	Oct-22	Nov-22	Dec-22
5	Mom	0.6	0.4					0.7	0.2	0.7	0.2	0.1	0.4
6	Dad	1.0	0.9					0.9	0.8	0.8	0.8	0.9	0.9
7	Helen	2.2	2.3					2.4	2.2	2.2	2.1	2.3	2.6
8	Max	2.0	1.7					1.7	1.7	1.6	1.5	1.8	1.9
9	Alexander	1.6	1.5	1.9		1.8	1.8	1.8	1.6	1.5	1.8	1.5	1.6
10													
11		Jan-23	Feb-23	Mar-23	Apr-23	May-23	Jun-23	Jul-23	Aug-23	Sep-23	Oct-23	Nov-23	Dec-23
12	Mom	1.1	0.9	0.8	0.8	1.1	0.6	0.4	1.1	0.6	1.0	0.7	0.9
13	Dad	1.2	1.1	1.2	0.8	0.7	1.3	1.1	0.7	0.7	0.8	1.0	1.0
14	Helen	2.2	2.5	2.3	2.0	2.6	1.5	1.5	2.0	2.3	1.7	2.6	2.8
15	Max	1.5	1.7	2.2	1.3	2.6	3.8	1.8	2.3	1.8	1.9	1.5	1.6
16	Alexander	2.2	1.7	1.8	2.4	2.1	2.3	1.9	2.1	2.3	2.8	2.1	1.6
17													

7.3.4   Moving cells between other cells

10. Look at the cells from A19 to A23.

19	Mom
20	Dad
21	Max
22	Helen
23	Alexander

Advice: There is a logical error in this cell area. The order of the family members differs from the order of the other two tables. Helen is older than Max and should therefore be above Max.

11. Select cell A22.

12. Point to the edge of the cell pointer with the mouse. However, do not point to the fill handle at the bottom right of the cell pointer.

Result: The mouse pointer is displayed with a cross consisting of four arrows ⛶.
Advice: This mouse pointer symbolizes the moving of cells. The fill handle, on the other hand, is only used to fill cells.

13. Press and hold the **shift key** ⇧.

14. Hold down the **shift key** ⇧ and drag the mouse upwards between cells A20 and A21. Pay attention to the green line.

15. First release the mouse button and then release the **shift key** ⇧.
Advice: The order of actions is crucial. If you were to release the shift key first, you would overwrite the cell. The green line indicates the new position of the cell. It is inserted between cells A20 and A21. The following cells are moved downwards.

16. Look at the result. Helen is inserted above Max.

7.3.5   Line breaks in cells

17. Select B18 and enter the word **Sum**. However, do not complete the entry yet.

18. Press the keyboard shortcut ⌑Alt⌑ + **enter key** ⌑↵⌑ to insert a manual line break.

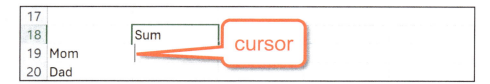

Advice: The input is <u>not</u> completed by this keyboard shortcut. The cursor is positioned in the second line of the cell. The following applies to all keyboard shortcuts: Press the first key and hold it down. Then briefly press the second key. Then release the first key again.

19. Enter **2022 + 2023** in the second line.

20. Press the **enter key** ⌑↵⌑ and look at the result.

Result: The entry is completed. The height of row 18 is doubled. It automatically adjusts to the content of this cell. The line break is also called text wrap.

21. Enter the heading **Average per month** in C18. Create another line break with ⌑Alt⌑ + **enter key** ⌑↵⌑ after **Average**.

7.3.6   Sums with two areas

In the range from B19 to B23, the values of both years per person should be added together.

22. Enter the formula **=SUM(B5:M5,B12:M12)** in cell B19.

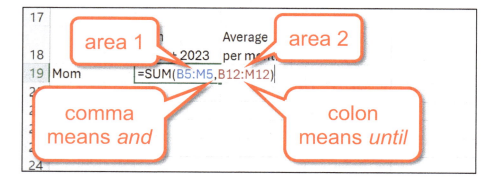

Advice: The sum function is used to add two areas. The colon (:) means *to*. The comma (,) means *and*. The formula there reads as follows: Add the areas B5 to M5 and B12 to M12.

23. Confirm the entry.

7.3.7   Copying formulas automatically

24. Select cell B19. Double-click on the fill handle to automatically copy the formula to the cells below.

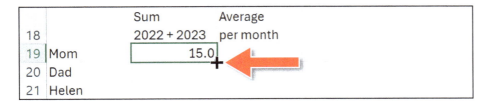

Advice: Double-clicking automatically fills subsequent cells.

7.3.8   Calculating the average with two areas

From C19 to C23, the average values of the years per person are to be calculated.

25. Enter the formula **=AVERAGE(B5:M5,B12:M12)** in cell C19.

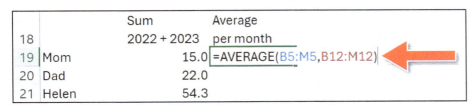

Advice: This formula differs from the previous one only by the function word **AVERAGE**. Again, the areas B5 to M5 and B12 to M12 are evaluated.

26. Complete the entry and copy the formula to the cells below.

7.3.9   AutoSum button

Until now, you have always typed in functions by hand. In this way, you have certainly learned the basic principle of functions. With the **AutoSum** button, you can also have the SUM function be entered automatically.

27. Select the cells B19 to C24.

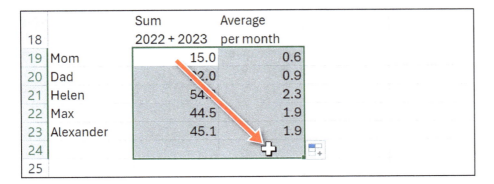

Advice: There are various ways to select the area for the AutoSum. In some cases, however, this can lead to undesirable results. If you select the values (B19 to C23) <u>and</u> the corresponding result cells (B24 and C24) as described in the instructions, no errors can occur when calculating the total. Possible errors are described in the following books.

28. Click on the **AutoSum** button $\boxed{\Sigma}$. Do <u>not</u> click on the arrow $\boxed{\vee}$ next to the button.

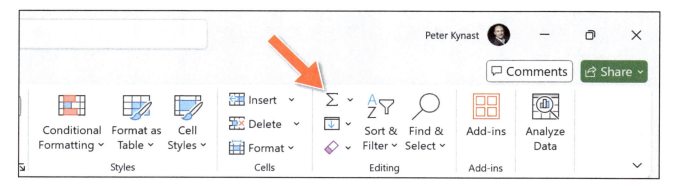

Result: The sums of the two columns are automatically calculated in cells B24 and C24.

7.3.10   Checking the formula

29. Select B24 and activate edit mode by pressing the **function key** $\boxed{F2}$ to check the formula.

		Sum	Average
18		2022 + 2023	per month
19	Mom	15.0	0.6
20	Dad	22.0	0.9
21	Helen	54.3	2.3
22	Max	44.5	1.9
23	Alexander	45.1	1.9
24		=SUM(B19:B23)	
25			

Or: You can also activate edit mode by double-clicking on the cell.

30. Exit edit mode by pressing the **enter key** $\boxed{\hookleftarrow}$ or the **escape key** $\boxed{Esc}$.
    Advice: As you have not made any changes, it makes no difference whether you exit edit mode with Enter or Escape.

7.3.11   Formats

31. Format the area A18 to C18 with the formats: **Bold**, **Center**, Fill color **Orange, Accent 2, Lighter 60%**
    Advice: The **Format Painter** button is not helpful in this situation. If you were to copy the format of cell B11 to A18 to C18, you would overwrite the existing text wrap in B18 and C18. Text wrap is a format. Text wrap is not cell content. As rows 4 and 11 are not formatted with a line break, you would overwrite the existing line break in cells B18 and C18. Text wrap is also called line break.

32. Format the area from A19 to C23 with **All Borders** $\boxed{\boxplus}$.

7.3.12   Conclusion

33. Save the file and close Excel.

8   Exercise: University sports festival

This exercise serves as a learning check and is the conclusion of the first section. Unlike instructions, the solution is not described here. You can see an illustration of the finished table on the right side.

8.1   Contents

- functions: MIN, MAX, AVERAGE
- formatting
- copying and pasting

8.2   Exercise

1. Open the sample file **Chapter 08 - University sports festival - Start - B2** and enable editing.
2. Set two decimal places for the times of the first run.
3. Determine the fastest participant of the first run in cell B15. Select the cell range using the pointing method.
4. In cell B16, determine the slowest participant in the first run.
5. Determine the average of all times of the first run in cell B17.
6. Copy the formulas from the first run to the second and third runs.
7. Use F15 to F17 to add the right border that was deleted during copying.
8. Correct the name in cell A10.
9. Set the headings in cells B5, D5 and F5 to align right.
10. Create multiple selections with the **control key** Ctrl and format the lines 6, 8, 10 and 12 with the fill color **Green, Accent 6, Lighter 60%**.
11. Double the height of row 14 to the value 30 (40 pixels).
12. Arrange the text in cell A14 vertically centered.
13. Save the file and close Excel.

	A	B	C	D	E	F
1	University sports festival					
2	Running results in seconds					
3	100-meter dash					
4						
5	Name	Run 1	Name	Run 2	Name	Run 3
6	Williams	13.24	Johnson	11.66	Smith	12.58
7	Garcia	11.21	Jones	10.95	Brown	11.49
8	Rodriguez	11.40	Davis	12.13	Moore	13.41
9	Anderson	13.31	Wilson	12.48	Martinez	12.43
10	Miller	11.52	Taylor	12.07	Thomas	13.52
11	Lee	12.26	Martin	12.23	Jackson	11.16
12	Perez	12.83	Thomson	12.31	White	11.17
13	Clark	13.35	Sanchez	11.69	Harris	11.60
14	Results					
15	Fastest	11.21		10.95		11.16
16	Slowest	13.35		12.48		13.52
17	Average	12.39		11.94		12.17
18						

Result: University sports festival

Compare!

Would you like to compare your exercises? You can find the result files in your sample file folder.

Section 2

Instructions

Contents of this section:

- differences between cell contents and cell formats
- number formats: fraction, percentage, date, time
- calculating with dates and times
- calculating with percentages
- filling several cells at the same time

9   Instruction: Contents and formats

The following instructions will provide you with important basic knowledge on the subject of cell contents and cell formats. In contrast to the other instructions, this exercise is not based on a specific practical example. It is purely an exercise table.

This chapter is particularly important for a basic understanding of Excel! It is therefore very important to review these instructions.

9.1   New content

- differences between cell contents and cell formats
- number formats: fraction, percentage, date and time
- calculating with dates and times
- selecting entire tables
- deleting all formats

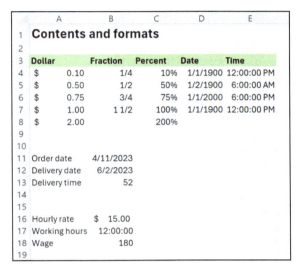

Result: Contents and formats

9.2   Repetition

- adapting column widths to a specific cell

9.3   Instruction

9.3.1   Opening the sample file

1. Open the sample file **Chapter 09 - Contents and formats - Start - B2** and enable editing.

9.3.2   Dollar format

2. Take a look at cell A4. The content of the cell is the value **0.1**.

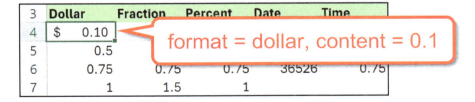

3. Select the cell and set the format to **dollar** $\boxed{\$}$.
4. Look at cell A4 again.

3	Dollar	Fraction	Percent	Date	Time
4	$ 0.10				
5	0.5		format = dollar, content = 0.1		
6	0.75	0.75	0.75	36526	0.75
7	1	1.5	1		

Advice: The content has not been changed! The format only changes the display of the content. What Excel displays is always the combination of the cell content and the cell format.

5. Select the area A5 to A8 and format these numbers with **dollar** $\boxed{\$}$ as well.

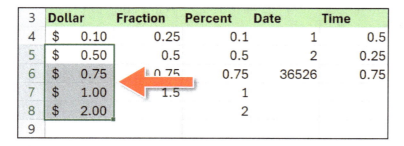

3	Dollar		Fraction	Percent	Date	Time
4	$	0.10	0.25	0.1	1	0.5
5	$	0.50	0.5	0.5	2	0.25
6	$	0.75	0.75	0.75	36526	0.75
7	$	1.00	1.5	1		
8	$	2.00		2		
9						

Advice: You probably expected this result. It therefore does not need to be explained any further.

9.3.3   Fraction format

6. Select cell B4.

7. Click on the arrow $\boxed{\vee}$ of the **Number Format** list box to open the list box.

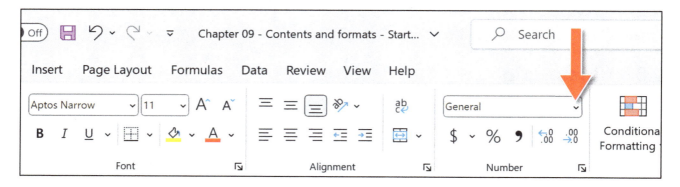

8. Click on the **Fraction** list item in the list box to set this number format.

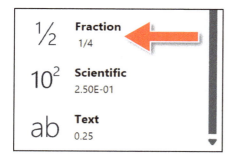

9. Look at the result.

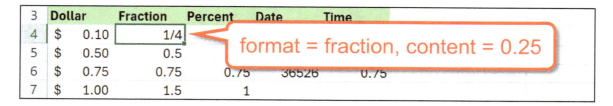

format = fraction, content = 0.25

Result: The value 0.25 is displayed as a fraction. However, the content has <u>not</u> changed! The content is still the value 0.25. It is just displayed differently using the **fraction** format.

10. Select B5 to B7 and format these numbers with the *fraction* format as well.

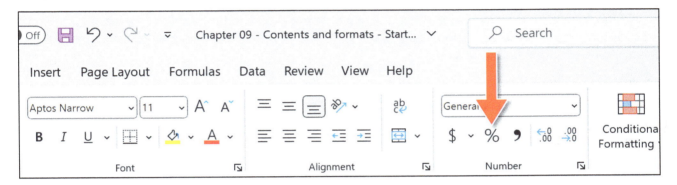

Result: The numbers are displayed as fractions. The contents have <u>not</u> changed.

9.3.4   Percent format

11. Select C5 and click on the *Percent* button % to assign this format.

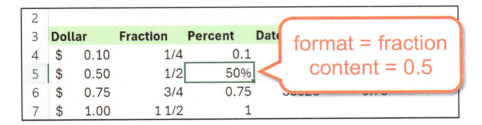

12. Look at the result.

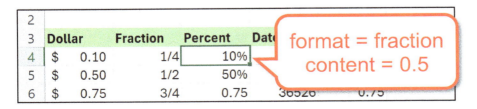

Result: The value 0.5 is displayed as a percentage of 50 %.
Advice: The value 0.5 corresponds to the value 50 %. They are mathematically identical. Therefore, 0.5 becomes the percentage 50 % and not 0.5 %. 50 % and 0.5 % are two different methods of expressing half (of something). The cell content 0.5 remains unchanged during this process.

13. Also format C4 with the format *Percent* % .

Advice: The value 0.1 corresponds to the percentage value 10 %.

14. Also format cells C6 to C8 with the format **Percent** %.

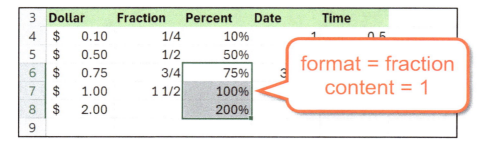

3	Dollar	Fraction	Percent	Date	Time
4	$ 0.10	1/4	10%	1	0.5
5	$ 0.50	1/2	50%		
6	$ 0.75	3/4	75%	3	
7	$ 1.00	1 1/2	100%		
8	$ 2.00		200%		
9					

format = fraction
content = 1

Advice: The value 0.75 corresponds to 75 %. The value 1 corresponds 100 % (1 whole = 100 %). The value 2 corresponds to 200 % (2 wholes = 200 %) etc.

9.3.5   Date format

Every date is a number! This number has a date format and therefore appears as a date. When you enter a date, a number is the content of the cell. By entering it as a date, Excel automatically assigns the date format. Excel's time calculation begins on 1/1/1900. 1/1/1900 corresponds to the number 1. In this case, the cell content is the value 1.

15. Select cell D7.

3	Dollar	Fraction	Percent	Date	Time
4	$ 0.10	1/4	10%	1	0.5
5	$ 0.50	1/2	50%	2	0.25
6	$ 0.75	3/4	75%	36526	0.75
7	$ 1.00	1 1/2	100%		
8	$ 2.00		200%		

16. Look at the **Number Format** list box.

Number Format list box

Advice: This list box shows the current number format of a cell. The number format **General** is the default setting for all cells.

17. Enter the date **1/1/1900** in cell D7.

5	$ 0.50	1/2	50%	2	0.25
6	$ 0.75	3/4	75%	36526	0.75
7	$ 1.00	1 1/2	100%	1/1/1900	
8	$ 2.00		200%		

18. Select cell D7 and look at the **Number Format** list box again.

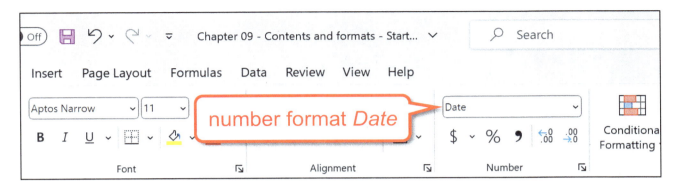

Result: The **Number Format** list box displays the **Date** format.

Advice: The following rules apply when working with dates in Excel:

• Every date is a number!
• When you enter a date, the format of the cell is automatically changed.
• Excel automatically sets the **Date** number format for this cell.
• The **Date** format displays this value as a date and not as a number.
• Excel's time calculation begins with the date 1/1/1900.
• The date 1/1/1900 corresponds to the value 1. 1/2/1900 corresponds to the value 2 and so on.

9.3.6 *Checking the number format*

19. Click on the arrow ⌄ of the **Number Format** list box to open the list box.

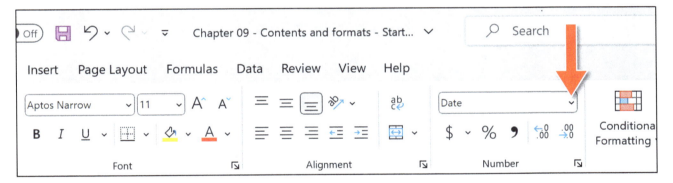

20. Click on the **General** list item to set the general number format for D7.

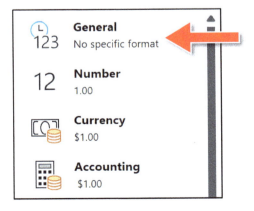

21. Look at the result.

4	$	0.10	1/4	10%	1	0.5
5	$	0.50	1/2	50%	2	0.25
6	$	0.75	3/4	75%	36526	
7	$	1.00	1 1/2	100%	1	
8	$	2.00		200%		

1 = content of the cell

Result: Cell D7 displays the value 1.

Advice: The first day of the Excel time calculation is 1/1/1900. The value 1 is the content of the cell! Date is the format. Both together result in the displayed date 1/1/1900. If the date format is removed, the numeric content of the cell can be seen

9.3.7   Cross-checking the number format

In the last step, the **Date** format was removed from cell D7. This made the content 1 visible. To carry out the cross-check, the format is reassigned below.

22. Click on the arrow ⌄ of the **Number Format** list box again to open the list box.

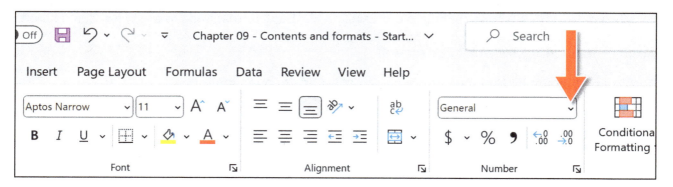

23. Click on the **short date** list item to set the date format again.

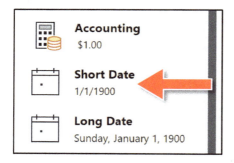

24. Look at the result.

5	$	0.50	1/2	50%	2	0.25
6	$	0.75	3/4	75%	36526	
7	$	1.00	1 1/2	100%	1/1/1900	
8	$	2.00		200%		

format = short date, content 1

Result: The value 1 is again displayed as the date 1/1/1900 using the date format.

Advice: A date is a number that is formatted as a date. For Excel, 1/1/1900 is day 1.

25. Select cells D4 to D6 and set the **short date** format for these cells in the **Number Format** list box.

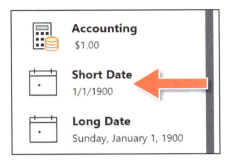

26. Look at the result.

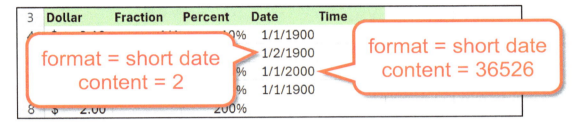

Advice: Each day corresponds to the value 1. Excel counts each day by the value 1. The number 2 is represented by the date format as 1/2/1900. The value 36526 is displayed as 1/1/2000 using the short date format. There are 100 years between 1/1/1900 and 1/1/2000. A year has 365 days. 100 x 365 = 36500. 26 leap years are added in this period. A leap year has one more day than a normal year. 36500 + 26 = 36526.

9.3.8   Consciously making mistakes

Mistakes cannot be avoided when learning. Sometimes it makes sense to consciously make a mistake in order to understand it better. In the following, you will incorrectly assign the euro format to cell D6.

27. Select cell D6 and assign the **dollar** $ format.

28. Look at the result.

3	Dollar	Fraction	Percent	Date	Time
4	$ 0.10	1/4	10%	1/1/1900	
5	$ 0.50	1/2	50%	1/2/1900	
6	$ 0.75	3/4	75%	$36,526.00	
7	$ 1.00	1 1/2	100%	1/1/1900	
8	$ 2.00		200%		

format = dollar
content = 36526

Advice: This result should no longer surprise you. The content of the cell was the value 36526 the whole time. Due to the date format, the number 36526 was first displayed as the date 1/1/2000. You then assigned the **dollar** format. Therefore the content is now displayed as a dollar amount of $ 36,526.00 and no longer as a date.

29. Click on the **Undo** button ↺ to replace the dollar format with the short date format.

9.3.9   Adapting the column width to a specific word.

30. Enter the following data in cells A11 to A13 and B11 to B12.

10		
11	Order date	4/11/2023
12	Delivery dat	6/2/2023
13	Delivery time	

Advice: The entries **Delivery date** and **Delivery time** do not fit inside their respective cell.

31. Select cell A13 and click on the **Format** button ⊞ Format ˅ .

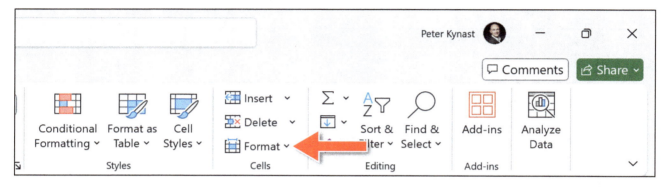

32. Click on **AutoFit Column Width** to adjust the width of column A to the cell content **Delivery time**.

Advice: Double-clicking on the dividing line between column headers A and B would adjust the width of the **Contents and formats** heading. In order for the width to be adjusted to a specific word, the word must be selected and the command **AutoFit Column Width** clicked.

9.3.10   Calculating with dates

Are you wondering what the background knowledge on dates is for? On the one hand, it will help you to better recognize and correct formatting errors. Another advantage is that you can calculate with dates.

33. Enter the formula **=B12-B11** in cell B13 to calculate the delivery time.

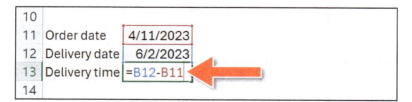

Advice: Every date is a number! To calculate the time between two dates, the dates are subtracted. 1/1/1900 is day 1 of the Excel time calculation. The order date (B11) is closer to 1/1/1900 than the delivery date. It is therefore the smaller number. The delivery date (B12) is the larger number. Therefore, calculate B12 minus B11.

34. Confirm the entry and look at the result.

Result: There are 52 days between the two dates.

Advice: The date 4/11/2023 is the 45027th day of the Excel time calculation. 6/2/2023 is the 45079th day. Excel calculates 45079 - 45027 = 52.

9.3.11   Time format

The same rules apply for the **Time** format as for the **Date** format. Every time entry is also a number! Each whole day (24 hours) corresponds to the value 1.

35. Select cell E7 and look at the **Number Format** list box.

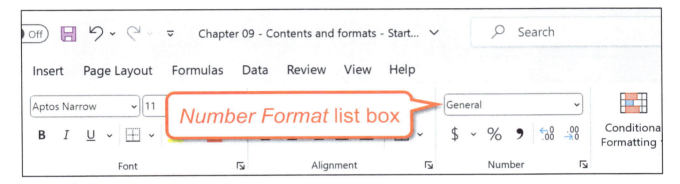

Advice: The **General** number format is active in this cell. This is the default setting for all cells.

36. Enter the time **12:00:00 PM** in cell E7.

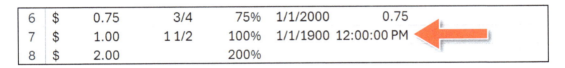

Advice: Times are noted with colons (:) in Excel.

37. Select cell E7 and look at the **Number Format** list box again.

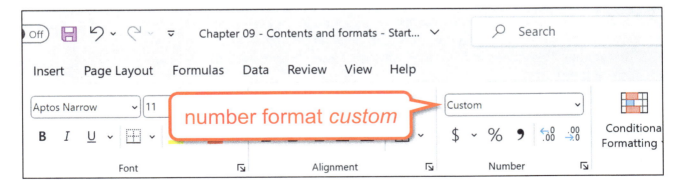

Advice: The term **Time** should actually appear here. Unfortunately, Excel is not consistent and logical at this point. **Custom** is a time format in this case! Therefore, replace the term **Custom** with the

term *Time* in your mind. Similar rules apply for the time format as for the date format.
- Every time is a number!
- This number is displayed as a time because the cell contains a time format.
- The time format is automatically assigned to the cell when it is entered.
- Each full day (24 hours) corresponds to the value 1. 12 hours = 0.5 etc.

9.3.12   Removing the time format

38. Click on the arrow ⌄ of the **Number Format** list box to open the list box.
39. Click on the **General** list item to delete the time format for E7 and set the general number format again.

40. Look at the result.

6	$	0.75	3/4	75%	1/1/2000	0.75
7	$	1.00	1 1/2	100%	1/1/1900	0.5
8	$	2.00		200%		

Result: Cell E7 displays the value 0.5.
Advice: The value 0.5 is the cell content. 12 hours correspond to half a day (0.5). By removing the time format, the unformatted content of the cell becomes visible.

41. Select cell E5. Click on the **Time** list item in the **Number Format** list box.

Date	Time
1/1/1900	0.5
1/2/1900	6:00:00 AM
1/1/2000	0.75

format = time, content = 0.25

Result: The value 0.25 is displayed as 06:00:00 AM.
Advice: The value 0.25 (one quarter) corresponds to six hours. Six hours is a quarter of a day. Due to the time format, the number 0.25 is displayed as 06:00:00 AM.

42. Format the other values in column E with the **Time** number format.
43. Look at the result.

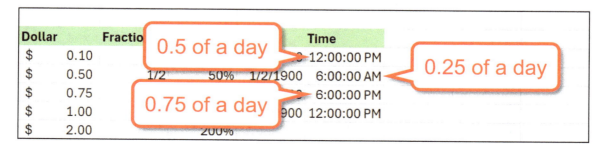

Dollar		Fractio			Time
$	0.10				12:00:00 PM
$	0.50	1/2	50%	1/2/1900	6:00:00 AM
$	0.75				6:00:00 PM
$	1.00			900	12:00:00 PM
$	2.00		200%		

0.5 of a day
0.25 of a day
0.75 of a day

9.3.13   Calculating with times

Times are also numbers. You can therefore also calculate with times. The following wage calculation contains a deliberate error at the beginning.

44. Enter the following data in cells A16 to A18 and B16 to B17. Adjust the width of column A to the cell content **working hours**. Do <u>not</u> add PM to 12:00:00. This time the 24-hour time format is used.

15		
16	Hourly rate	$ 15.00
17	Working hours	12:00:00
18	Wage	

45. Enter the formula **=B16*B17** in cell B18 to calculate the wage.

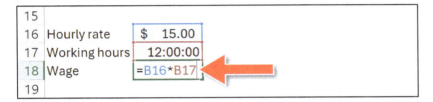

46. Confirm the entry and look at the result.

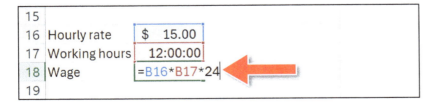

Result: The value 7.5 is output as a wage.

Advice: With the knowledge you have just acquired, you may be able to explain this result. Excel always calculates with the content of a cell! The format does not matter. The content of cell B17 is the value 0.5, so Excel calculates: **15 x 0.5 = 7.5**

9.3.14   Correcting the formula

To solve this issue, the factor 24 must be added to the formula. By multiplying by 24, any time in Excel can be converted into a normal number (decimal number). 12:00:00 becomes 12, 06:00:00 becomes 6, 18:00:00 becomes 18 and so on. This also applies to crooked times. For example, with the factor 24, 17:34:09 hours become the decimal number 17.56916667.

47. Select cell B18 again and press the **function key** F2 to activate edit mode for the cell.
48. Add the factor 24 to the formula: **=B16*B17*24**.

15		
16	Hourly rate	$ 15.00
17	Working hours	12:00:00
18	Wage	=B16*B17*24
19		

Advice: Factor means that a value is multiplied by this value. The factor 24 turns the value 12:00:00 (0.5) into the desired value 12. This multiplication also works with all other time values.

Examples:

12:00:00 = 0,5 | 0.5 x 24 = 12
06:00:00 = 0.25 | 0.25 x 24 = 6
18:00:00 = 0.75 | 0.75 x 24 = 18 etc.

To multiply times by normal numbers, a factor of 24 is added. This also applies to fractional times, e.g. 17:34:09.

49. Look at the result.

16	Hourly rate	$ 15.00
17	Working hours	12:00:00
18	Wage	180

Advice: Cells B16 and B17 have different number formats (dollar and time). Excel therefore does not assign either format to the result. The general number format is displayed instead.

9.3.15   Deleting formats

Sometimes it is helpful to delete all formats of one or more cells. This gives you a view of the pure content and may make it easier to find errors. To demonstrate this method, the formats are deleted from all cells below and then restored.

50. Click on the **table selector** [ ] at the top left to select the entire table.

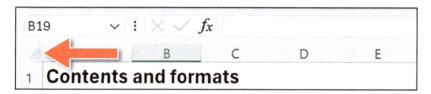

51. Click on the **Clear** button [◇ ˇ] to open the list box for this button.

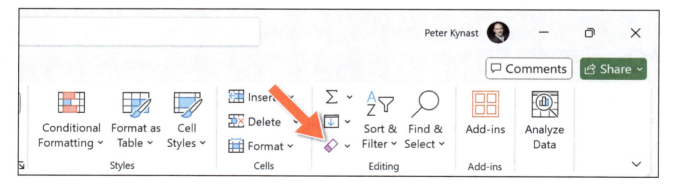

Advice: Depending on the size of your screen, the button may be displayed differently. On larger monitors, the **Clear** button is displayed with a label (see illustration on the next page).

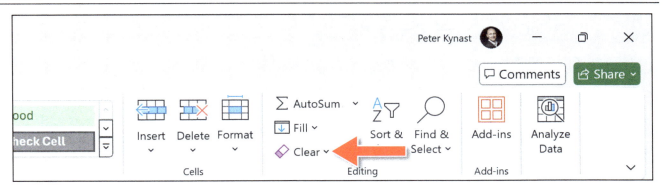

52. Click on the **Clear Formats** list item in the list box of the button.

53. Undo the selection and look at the result.

1	Contents and formats				
2					
3	Dollar	Fraction	Percent	Date	Time
4	0.1	0.25	0.1	1	0.5
5	0.5	0.5	0.5	2	0.25
6	0.75	0.75	0.75	36526	0.75
7	1	1.5	1	1	0.5
8	2		2		
9				no formats	
10					
11	Order date	45027			
12	Delivery date	45079			
13	Delivery time	52			
14					
15					
16	Hourly rate	15			
17	Working hours	0.5			
18	Wage	180			

Result: The formats for numbers, fonts and fill colors are deleted.
Advice: The formats are reverted to the general number format. This includes settings like font size, color, background color and borders. Resetting all formats is useful in many cases. This procedure can be helpful whenever Excel displays unexpected results. This allows you to see the actual content of the cell(s) and detect errors more easily.
Read more: Please also read Chapter 24 Explanation: Contents and formats, page 143.

54. Click on the **Undo** button ⟲ to restore the formats to their previous settings.

9.3.16 Conclusion
55. Save the file and close Excel.

10 Instruction: Letterheads

Use this guide to calculate the billing amount for an order of letterheads.

10.1 New content
- calculating with percentages
- entering cell references with the arrow keys (pointing method)

10.2 Repetitions
- thousands separator
- simple formulas
- entering percentage values

10.3 Instruction

10.3.1 Opening the sample file

1. Open the sample file **Chapter 10 - Letterheads - Start - B2** and enable editing.

10.3.2 Thousands separator format

2. Select cell B2. Click on the small arrow ⬒ at the bottom right of the Number group to open the **Format Cells** dialog box.

	A	B
1	Letterheads	
2	Amount	10,000
3	Net cost per 1000 pieces	$ 30.00
4	Subtotal	$ 300.00
5		
6	Quantity discount in percent	5%
7	Quantity discount in dollar	$ 15.00
8	Net price	$ 285.00
9		
10	Sales tax in percent	8%
11	Sales tax in dollar	$ 22.80
12	**Billing amount**	**$ 307.80**
13		

Result: Letterheads

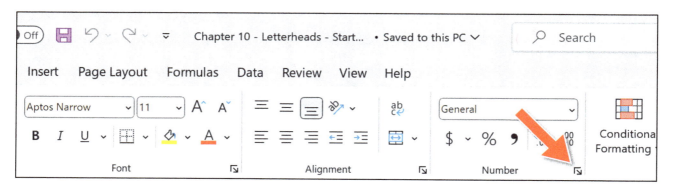

Advice: The Format cells dialog box is one of the most important dialog boxes in Excel. Almost all formats for cells can be switched on and off here. In addition to the method shown, there are other ways to open the Format Cells dialog box.

3. Click on the **Number** category in the **Numbers** tab to activate this category.

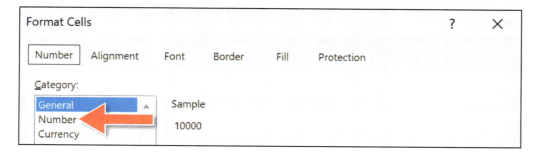

4. Make the following changes:
    • Decimal places: 0
    • Use 1000 Separator: activate (check box)

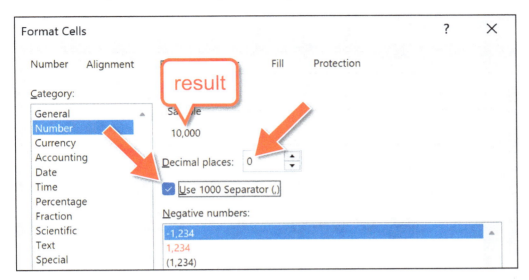

Advice: The example shows the result of the settings. It refers to the selected cell B2.

5. Click on the **OK** button to apply these settings.

Result: The number in B2 is displayed with the thousands separator (,). The thousands separator is a comma. It is placed after every third digit from the right to improve the legibility of a number. Larger numbers in particular, such as millions and billions, are easier for the eye to read in this way.

10.3.3   Determining the subtotal

6. Enter the formula **=B2/1000*B3** in B4 to determine the subtotal.

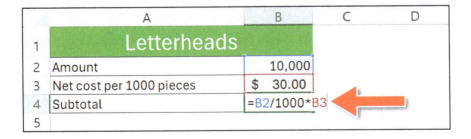

Advice: 1000 pieces cost $ 30.00. Therefore B2 is first divided by 1000 and then multiplied by B3. The following applies to Excel: If there is a value in the table, you should always refer to this value with a cell reference when making calculations. This ensures that your formula is automatically re-calculated if the value in the cell is changed once. The value 1000 does not exist in any cell, so it can be safely entered in the formula as a fixed value. Cell A3 cannot be used for calculations as there is text in the cell as well as the number. The content of this cell would be interpreted by Excel as text.

7. Look at the result.

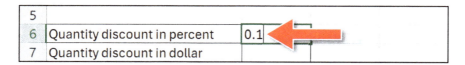

10.3.4   Entering a percentage

8. Enter the number **0.1** in cell B6.

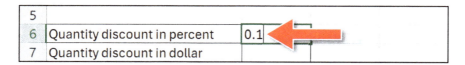

Advice: The value 0.1 corresponds to the percentage value 10 %.

9. Select cell B6 and click on the **Percent** button % to assign this format.

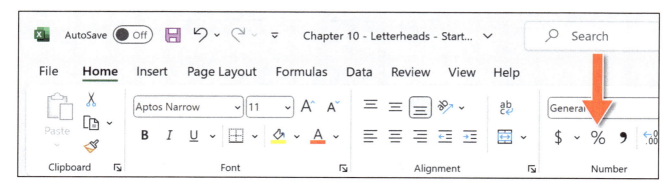

Result: The value 0.1 is displayed as a percentage of 10 %.
Or: When entering a percentage value, the percent sign can also be typed in directly. In this case, you can enter **10 %**. The subsequent formatting with the percent format is not necessary. Both methods lead to the same result.

10.3.5   Determining the quantity discount

10. Enter the formula **=B4*B6** in B7 to calculate the quantity discount in dollar.

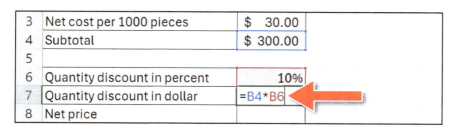

Advice: The content of cell B6 is the value 0.1. It makes no mathematical difference whether you calculate **300 x 0.1** or **300 x 10 %**. The two methods are identical and lead to the same result.

10.3.6   Determining the net price

11. Enter the formula **=B4-B7** in Cell B8 to calculate the sales price.

3	Net cost per 1000 pieces	$ 30.00
4	Subtotal	$ 300.00
5		
6	Quantity discount in percent	10%
7	Quantity discount in dollar	$ 30.00
8	Net price	=B4-B7
9		

Advice: One error occurs particularly frequently when working with Excel. Many users always use the SUM function for calculations. In this situation, it would look like this: **=SUM(B4-B7)**. This use of the SUM function is incorrect! Although it leads to the same result, the SUM function is unnecessary ballast. The calculation **=B4-B7** is already complete. Only use the SUM function if you really want to add. SUM stands for addition! This process involves subtraction.

10.3.7   Entering a percentage

12. Enter the value **8%** in cell B10. This time type the percent sign (%) using the keyboard and complete the entry.

8	Net price	$ 270.00
9		
10	Sales tax in percent	8%
11	Sales tax in dollar	
12	**Billing amount**	
13		

Advice: It makes no difference whether you enter 8 % or 0.08 and then format the cell with the number format **Percentage** %. The two methods are equivalent.

13. Select cell B10 and look at the **Number Format** list box to check the current number format.

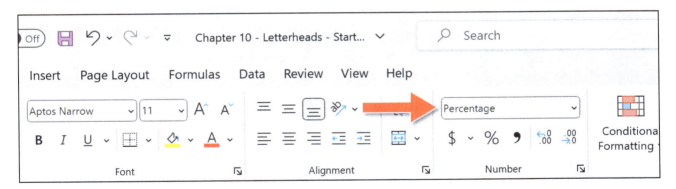

Result: The format **Percentage** has been assigned to cell B10 automatically.

10.3.8   Calculating the sales tax

14. Calculate the sales tax in B11. To do this, multiply the cells B8 and B10.

6	Quantity discount in percent	10%
7	Quantity discount in dollar	$ 30.00
8	Net price	$ 270.00
9		
10	Sales tax in percent	8%
11	Sales tax in dollar	=B8*B10
12	**Billing amount**	
13		

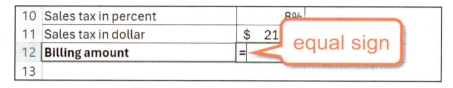

Advice: The price in cell B8 is a net price. It does not include the sales tax yet.

10.3.9   Determining the billing amount using the pointing method

15. Enter an equal sign (=) in cell B12. Do <u>not</u> press the **enter key** ⏎ yet.

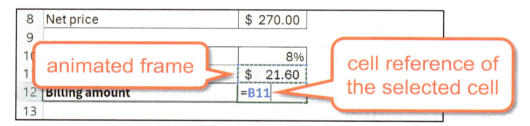

10	Sales tax in percent	8%
11	Sales tax in dollar	$ 21
12	**Billing amount**	=
13		

equal sign

16. Press the **up arrow key** ↑ on the keyboard once.

8	Net price	$ 270.00
9		
10		8%
11		$ 21.60
12	Billing amount	=B11
13		

animated frame

cell reference of the selected cell

Result: An animated frame appears. It highlights the cell B11. The corresponding cell reference B11 is entered in B12.
Advice: The arrow keys are sometimes also referred to as **cursor keys**.
Attention: Do not confuse the **up arrow key** with the **shift key**.

17. Press the **up arrow** key ↑ three more times to select B8.

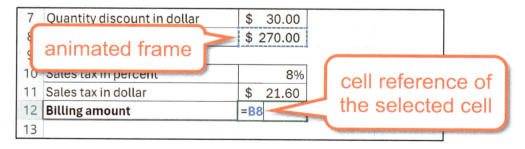

7	Quantity discount in dollar	$ 30.00
8		$ 270.00
9		
10	Sales tax in percent	8%
11	Sales tax in dollar	$ 21.60
12	**Billing amount**	=B8
13		

animated frame

cell reference of the selected cell

Result: The animated frame is located on cell B8. The corresponding cell reference is entered into the formula.

18. Enter a plus sign (+).

10	Sales tax in percent	8%
11	Sales tax in dollar	$ 21.60
12	**Billing amount**	=B8+
13		
14		

plus

Result: The animated frame is no longer visible.

19. Press the **up arrow** key ↑ to select B11.

10	Sales tax in percent	8%
11	Sales tax in dollar	$ 21.60
12	**Billing amount**	=B8+B11
13		

Result: The animated frame appears again and highlights cell B11. The cell reference of this cell is copied to the formula.

20. Confirm the entry and look at the result.

10	Sales tax in percent	8%
11	Sales tax in dollar	$ 21.60
12	**Billing amount**	**$ 291.60**
13		
14		

Result: The billing amount is $ 291.60 and consists of the net price and the sales tax. Prices that include the sales tax are also referred to as gross prices.

10.3.10 *Changing the percentage values*

If a percentage is to be changed, the new percentage value can be entered directly into the cell without a percent sign.

21. Select cell B6 and enter the value 5.

2	Amount	10,000
3	Net cost per 1000 pieces	$ 30.00
4	Subtotal	$ 300.00
5		
6	Quantity discount in percent	5%
7	Quantity discount in dollar	$ 30.00
8	Net price	$ 270.00

Result: The **Percentage** format is already active in the cell. It no longer needs to be entered. The percent sign also remains visible during edit mode.

22. Confirm the entry.

10.3.11 *Conclusion*

23. Save the file and close Excel.

11   Instruction: Solar power plant

Use this guide to calculate the project costs for a solar power plant.

11.1   New content

- preventing automatic formatting with an apostrophe
- filling several cells at the same time
- wrapping text inside a cell

11.2   Repetitions

- Auto Fill Options
- moving cells between other cells
- single cell minus sum of an area
- AutoSum button
- sum of two areas
- calculating with percentages and dates

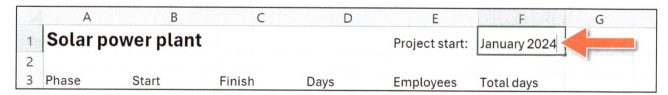

Result: Solar power plant

11.3   Instruction

11.3.1   Opening the sample file

1. Open the sample file **Chapter 11 - Solar power plant - Start - B2** and enable editing.

11.3.2   Preventing automatic formatting using an apostrophe

Excel has a number of automatic functions that are often helpful but sometimes also annoying. For example, a date with the spelling **January 2024** is automatically shortened to **Jan-24** and converted to the date format.

2. Enter the text **January 2024** in F1.

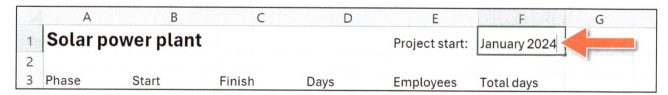

3. Confirm the entry and look at the result.

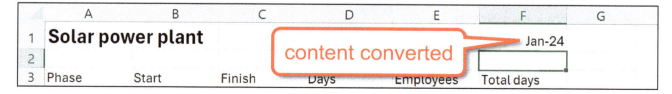

Advice: The entry is automatically changed when you confirm. **January 2024** becomes **Jan-24** and is converted into the **date** format. This automatic change is initially irritating. However, it can easily be prevented.

4.   Enter the text **'January 2024** in cell F1. Overwrite the old cell content and pay attention to the single preceding apostrophe (').

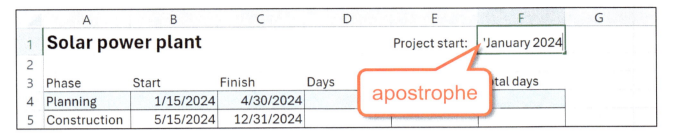

Attention: You need to use the **apostrophe key** ['] next to the **enter key** [↵]. Using the **accent key** [`] will not work as intended in this situation.

5.   Confirm the entry and look at the result.

Result: The input is not changed. The apostrophe (') is not visible. However, it is part of the cell content! If you enter the edit mode of cell F1, the apostrophe becomes visible again.

11.3.3   Calculating the days between to dates

6.   Enter the formula **=C4-B4** in cell D4 to calculate the number of days between the two dates.

2						
3	Phase	Start	Finish	Days	Employees	Total days
4	Planning	1/15/2024	4/30/2024	=C4-B4	4	
5	Construction	5/15/2024	12/31/2024			

Advice: To calculate the period between two dates, the two dates are subtracted. Each date is a number! The date that is closer to 1/1/1900 is the smaller number. In this calculation, this is the start date in B4. C4 is the larger number. Therefore, calculate C4 minus B4.

7.   Confirm the entry and look at the result.

3	Phase	Start	Finish	Days	Employees	Total days
4	Planning	1/15/2024	4/30/2024	106	4	
5	Construction	5/15/2024	12/31/2024			
6	Elec. devices	1/1/2025	6/30/2025			

Result: There are 106 days between the two dates.

8.   Copy the formula in D4 to cells D5 to D7 using the black cross ✚.

3	Phase	Start	Finish	Days	Employees	Total days
4	Planning	1/15/2024	4/30/2024	106	4	
5	Construction	5/15/2024	12/31/2024			
6	Elec. devices	1/1/2025	6/30/2025			

9. Look at the result.

3	Phase	Start	Finish	Days	Employees	Total days
4	Planning	1/15/2024	4/30/2024	106	4	
5	Construction	5/15/2024	12/31/2024	230		
6	Elec. devices	1/1/2025	6/30/2025	180		
7	Completio		25	122		
8						
9	Position	Planning	Elec. devices	Construction	Completion	Sums

fill color blue → *Auto Fill Options*

Result: Cells D5 to D7 are overwritten by using the fill function. They receive the blue fill color from cell D4. The **Auto Fill Options** button appears at the bottom right of the selection.

Advice: As long as the selection is active, the blue color is not clearly visible. If you undo the selection, the uniform color of the four cells from D4 to D7 is easier to see.

10. Click on the **Auto Fill Options** button to open the list box.

6	Elec. devices	1/1/2025	6/30/2025	180		
7	Completion	7/1/2025	10/31/2025	122		
8						
9	Position	Planning	Elec. devices	Construction	Completion	Sums

11. Click on the **Fill Without Formatting** list item to copy only the formula and not the formatting.

7	Completion	7/1/2025	10/31/2025	122	
8					
9	Position	Planning	Elec. devices	Construction	◉ Copy Cells
10	**Budget**	65000	42,000,000	37,500,000	○ Fill Formatting Only
11	Staff				○ Fill Without Formatting ←
12	Material	10,000	2,400,000		○ Flash Fill
13	Energy	500	24,000		
14	Machines	0	40,200,000		3,000,000

12. Look at the result. The fill color has been removed from cells D5 and D7.

2						
3	Phase	Start	Finish	Days	Employees	Total days
4	Planning	1/15/2024	4/30/2024	106	4	
5	Construction	5/15/2024	12/31/2024	230		
6	Elec. devices	1/1/2025	6/30/2025	180		
7	Completion	7/1/2025	10/31/2025	122		
8						
9	Position	Planning	Elec. devices	Construction	Completion	Sums

fill color removed

11.3.4 Filling several cells at the same time

Cells E5 to E7 should be filled with the same value in one step.

13. Select cells E5 to E7 and look at cell E5 and the name field.

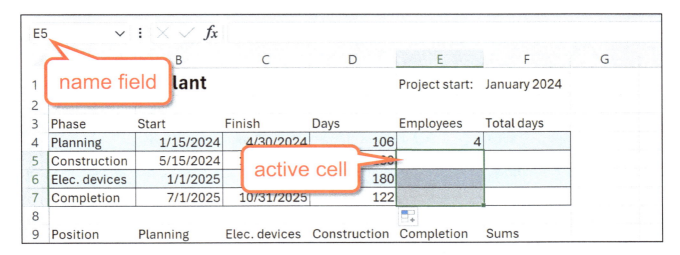

Result: E5 and E7 have no fill color. As E5 is the active cell, it is displayed in a lighter color than E7. The name field shows the name of the active cell.

Advice: In a selection, one cell is <u>always</u> the active cell. The selection is transparent at this point. It is not darkened. The active cell is the cell that receives your keyboard input.

14. Enter the value **25**. However, do <u>not</u> press the **enter key** [↵] yet.

4	Planning	1/15/2024	4/30/2024	106	4	
5	Construction	5/15/2024	12/31/2024	230	25	
6	Elec. devices	1/1/2025	6/30/2025	180		
7	Completion	7/1/2025	10/31/2025	122		
8						

Result: As E5 is the active cell in the selection, the entry is made in this cell.

15. Confirm the entry with the key combination **control key** [Ctrl] + **enter key** [↵] to fill the three cells simultaneously. Look at the result.

4	Planning	1/15/2024	4/30/2024	106	4	
5	Construction			230	25	
6	Elec. devices			180	25	
7	Completion			122	25	
8						

filled in at the same

Read more: Please also read Chapter 26 Explanation: Keyboard shortcuts, page 146.

11.3.5   Calculating the total number of days

16. Enter the formula **=D4*E4** in cell F4 to calculate the total working days for planning.

3	Phase	Start	Finish	Days	Employees	Total days
4	Planning	1/15/2024	4/30/2024	106	4	=D4*E4
5	Construction	5/15/2024	12/31/2024	230	25	

17. Confirm the entry and copy the formula to the following cells.
    Result: As in column D, the blue fill color from cell F4 is copied to the other cells as well.

18. Click on the **Auto Fill Options** button to open the list box.

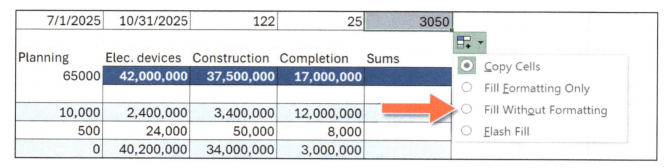

19. Click on the **Fill Without Formatting** list item to copy only the formula and not the blue fill color.

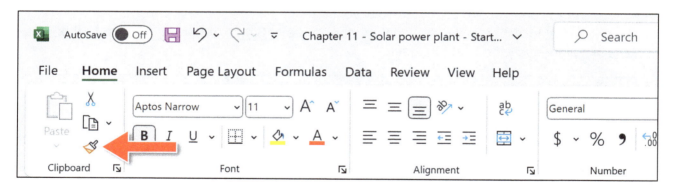

11.3.6   Copying the formatting using the format painter

20. Select cell F3 and set the alignment to **Align Right**.

21. Select the cells A3 to F3 and set the format to **Bold**. Leave these cells selected.

22. Click on the **Format Painter** button to activate this tool.

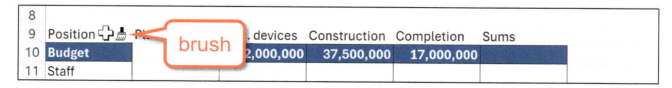

Result: The selected cells are highlighted with an animated frame.

23. Point the mouse at cell A9 and look at the mouse pointer.

Result: A brush is displayed next to the white cross. This brush symbolizes the active **Format Painter** tool.

24. Click on cell A9 to copy the formats to this position. Look at the result.

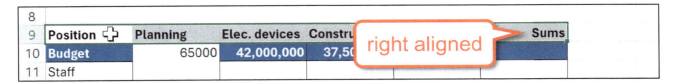

Result: The formats of the area from A3 to F3 are copied to cells A9 to F9. The **Align Right** format from cell F3 has also been copied to cell F9.

25. Select C10 and click on the **Format Painter** button  again.
26. Click on cell B10 to copy the format from C10 to B10.

11.3.7   Merging cells and wrapping text

27. Enter the following text in cell H4: **Due to urgency, the project has received an exemption for Sunday work.**

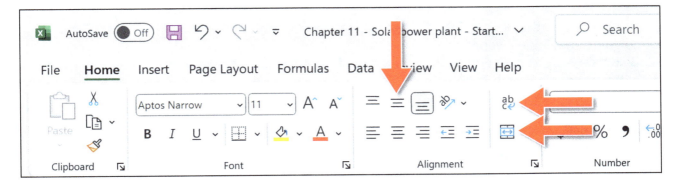

28. Select the cells H4 to K7 and click on the **Merge & Center** button [⬚], the **Wrap Text** button [ab cↄ] and the **Middle Align** button [≡].

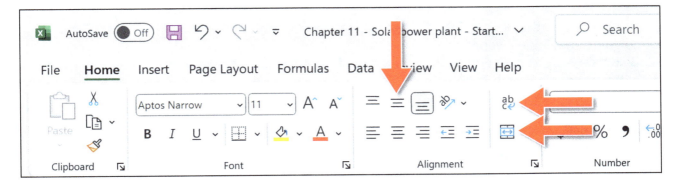

Advice: You have already used the **Merge & Center** format several times. You should be familiar with it. What is new in this situation is that the connection of the cells is created over several lines. The **Wrap Text** format wraps the text within the cell. **Middle Align** aligns the text <u>vertically</u> in the middle.

29. Look at the result.

Employees	Total days
4	424
25	5750
25	4500
25	3050

H4 → Due to urgency, the project has received an exemption for Sunday work.

Advice: The name of the large and connected cell is H4. It is based on the first cell at the top left of the connected cell.

30. Also set the following formats: **Font Size 14**, **Thick Outside Borders**, fill color: **Dark Blue, Text 2, Lighter 90%**

11.3.8 Swapping columns

31. Look at cells A5 and A6 and compare the order of the contents with cells C9 and D9.

	Phase	Start	Finish	Days	Employees	Total days
3	Phase	Start	Finish	Days	Employees	Total days
4	Planning	1/15/2024	4/30/2024	106	4	424
5	Construction					5750
6	Elec. devices					4500
7	Completion	7/1/2025	10/31/2025	122	25	3050
8						

construction, electrical devices

	Position	Planning	Elec. devices	Construction	Completion	Sums
9	Position	Planning	Elec. devices	Construction	Completion	Sums
10	Budget	65,000	42,000,000	37,500,000	17,000,000	
11	Staff					
12	Material				00	
13	Energy				00	
14	Machines	0	40,200,000	34,000,000	3,000,000	

electrical devices, construction

Advice: The order of cells C9 and D9 does not correspond to the order of the cells A5 and A6. The columns should be swapped.

32. Select cells C9 to C14 and point to the edge of the selection with the mouse. However, do <u>not</u> point to the fill handle on the bottom right.

	Position	Planning	Elec. devices	Construction	Completion	Sums
8						
9	Position	Planning	Elec. devices	Construction	Completion	Sums
10	Budget	65,000	42,000,000	37,50...	17,000,000	
11	Staff					
12	Material	10,000	2,400,000	3,4...		
13	Energy	500	24,000	50,000	8,000	
14	Machines	0	40,200,000	34,000,000	3,000,000	
15						
16	Difference					

mouse pointer

Result: The mouse pointer is displayed with a cross consisting of four arrows 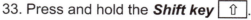.

33. Press and hold the **Shift key** ⇧ .

34. Drag the mouse between columns D and E. Pay attention to the green line.

8						
9	**Position**	**Planning**	**Elec. devices**	**Construction**	Comp...	ns
10	**Budget**	65,000	42,000,000	37,500,000	17,0...	
11	Staff					
12	Material	10,000	2,400,000	3,400,000	12,000,000	
13	Energy	500	24,000	50,000		
14	Machines	0	40,200,000	34,000,000		
15						
16	**Difference**					

> green line
> mouse pointer

Advice: The green line indicates the new position of the area.
Attention: Make sure that the green line is exactly at the position shown and that the line is displayed vertically. Otherwise the area will be inserted in the wrong position.

35. First release the mouse button and then the **shift key** ⇧ .
    Attention: The order is crucial! If you release the shift key first, the electrical devices section will be moved <u>to</u> the construction section. You would overwrite the construction section. A message would first appear asking you whether you want to replace the cells.

36. Look at the result. The two columns have been swapped.

8						
9			Construction	Elec. devices		
10			000	37,500,000	42,000,000	1
11	Staff					
12	Material	10,000	3,400,000	2,400,000	12,000,000	
13	Energy	500	50,000	24,000	8,000	
14	Machines	0	34,000,000	40,200,000	3,000,000	
15						

> construction
> electrical devices

11.3.9   Calculation of staff costs

37. Enter the formula **=F4*65*8** in B11 to calculate the staff costs for the planning area.

9	**Position**	**Planning**	**Construction**	**Elec. devices**	**Completion**	**Sums**
10	**Budget**	65,000	37,500,000	42,000,000	17,000,000	
11	Staff	=F4*65*8				
12	Material	10,000	3,400,000	2,400,000	12,000,000	
13	Energy	500	50,000	24,000	8,000	
14	Machines	0	34,000,000	40,200,000	3,000,000	
15						

Advice: The hourly rate for engineers in the planning department is $ 65. The daily work time is eight hours. As these two figures do not appear in the table, they are entered as fixed values in the formula. However, as soon as a value appears in a cell, you should always refer to this cell with a cell reference! In this way, you ensure that the formula calculates with the new number if the value is changed.

38. Enter the formula **=F5*29*8** to calculate the staff costs for the construction.

9	Position	Planning	Construction	Elec. devices	Completion	Sums
10	Budget	65,000	37,500,000	42,000,000	17,000,000	
11	Staff	220,480	=F5*29*8			
12	Material	10,000	3,400,000	2,400,000	12,000,000	
13	Energy	500	50,000	24,000	8,000	

Advice: The hourly rate for construction, electrical devices and completion work is $ 29. The daily work time for these three areas is eight hours. These values are also not available as separate cells in the table. They can therefore be safely used as fixed values in the formula. If you ever change the table and enter the hourly wages or working hours in separate cells, you should also change the formula in C11 and use cell references to refer to the cells with the hourly wages and working hours.

11.3.10 Consciously making mistakes

In this situation, one error is especially common. As the hourly rates and working hours in the areas of construction, electrical devices and completion are the same, it seems to make sense to copy the formula from C11 to cells D11 and E11 using the fill function. As the formula is copied horizontally in this situation while the total days are arranged vertically, an error occurs. For demonstration purposes, this error is deliberately recreated below.

39. Select C11 and copy the formula from C11 to D11 and E11.

9	Position	Planning	Construction	Elec. devices	Completion	Sums
10	Budget	65,000	37,500,000	42,		
11	Staff	220,480	1,334,000	mouse pointer		
12	Material	10,000	3,400,000	2,		
13	Energy	500	50,000	24,000	8,000	

40. Look at the result. The value 0 is displayed in D11 and E11.

9	Position	Planning	Construction	Elec. devices	Completion	Sums
10	Budget	65,000	37,500,000	42,000,000	17,000,000	
11	Staff	220,480	1,334,000	0	0	
12	Material	10,000	3,400,000	2,400,000	12,000,000	
13	Energy	500	50,000	24,000	8,000	

41. Select D11 and press the **function key** F2 to activate edit mode.

9	Position	Planning	Construction	Elec. devices	Completion	Sums
10	Budget	65,000	37,500,000	42,000,000	17,000,000	
11	Staff	220,480	1,334,000	=G5*29*8	0	
12	Material	10,000	3,400,000	400,000	12,000,000	
13	Energy	500	50		000	
14	Machines	0	34,000	F5 becomes G5	000	
15						

Result: The reference F5 from cell C11 has been changed to G5.

Advice: When filling formulas horizontally, Excel always changes the letters of the cell references! However as the total days are arranged vertically, the formula must be **=F6*29*8**.

42. Correct the formulas in D11 and E11.

11.3.11 Calculating sums with the AutoSum button

43. Select the cells B10 to F14.

44. Click on the **AutoSum** button $\boxed{\Sigma}$ to calculate the sums automatically.

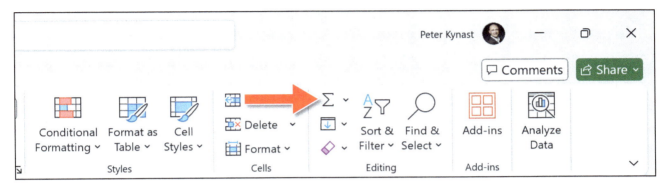

Result: The sums are entered in the cells F10 to F14.

45. Select cell F10 and look at the name field and the formula bar.

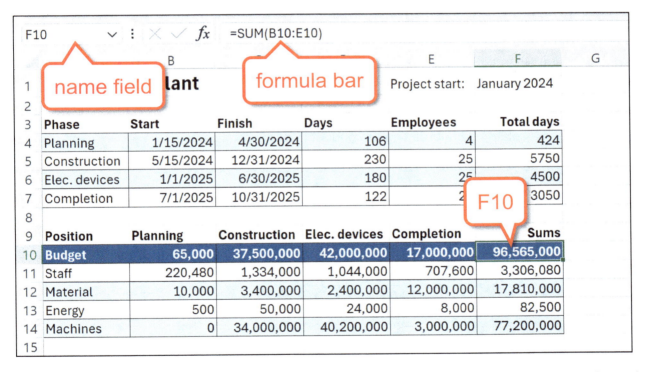

Advice: F10 is the active cell. As F10 has a dark fill color, it is not easily recognizable as the active cell. In such cases, it is helpful to look at the name field. It shows the active cell. The content of the active cell is displayed in the formula bar. Whether you type in the SUM function by hand or use the **AutoSum** button is up to your preference. Both procedures lead to the same result.

11.3.12 Deleting rows

46. Click on the row header of row 15 to select row 15.

13	Energy	500	50,000	24,000	8,000	82,500
14	Machines	0	34,000,000	40,200,000	3,000,000	77,200,000
15						
16	**Difference**					
17						

Advice: When you click on a row header, the mouse is displayed as a black arrow ➡.

47. Click on the **Delete** button [⊟× Delete ⌄] to delete the row. Do <u>not</u> click on the small arrow [⌄] next to the button.

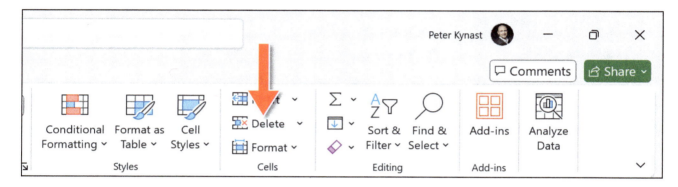

Advice: The basic rule applies: When you click the **Delete** button, the cells that are currently selected are deleted. Since an entire row is selected, the entire row is also deleted.

11.3.13 Calculating the difference

The difference is calculated by subtracting the budget from the total costs.

48. Enter the formula **=B10-SUM(B11:B14)** in B15 to calculate the difference.

9	**Position**	**Planning**	**Construction**	**Elec. devices**	**Completion**	**Sums**
10	**Budget**	6⋯	⋯0,000	42,000,000	17,000,000	96,565,000
11	Staff	2⋯	⋯4,000	1,044,000	707,600	3,306,080
12	Material	1⋯	⋯0,000	2,400,000	12,000,000	17,810,000
13	Energy	500	50,000	24,000	8,000	82,500
14	Machines	0	34,000,000	40,200,000	3,000,000	77,200,000
15	Difference	=B10-SUM(B11:B14)				
16						
17	⋯ machines					
18	⋯					
19	Buffer in %					
20	Buffer in $					
21	Upper limit					

budget — minus — sum of costs

Advice: The budget is noted in cell B10. The costs result from adding the cells B11 to B14. This results in the formula **=B10-SUM(B11:B14)**.

49. Copy the formula in B15 to the adjacent cells C15 to F15.

11.3.14 Adding up the costs for machines and material

Material and machinery must be purchased and stored. In order to better plan storage costs and capacities, the construction company evaluates these two items separately.

50. Enter the formula **=SUM(B12:E12,B14:E14)** in B18 to add up all costs for materials and machines. Pay attention to the color highlighting of the areas.

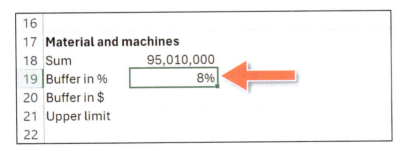

9	Position	Planning	Construction	Elec. devices	Completion	Sums
10	Budget	65,000	37,500,000	42,000,000	17,000,000	96,565,000
11	Staff	220,480	1,334,000	1,044,000	707,600	3,
12	Material	10,000	3,400,000	2,400,000	12,000,000	
13	Energy	500	50,000	24,000	8,000	82,500
14	Machin	0	34,000,000	40,200,000	3,000,000	
15	Differe	65,980	-1,284	,000	1,284,400	-1,
16						
17	Material and machi					
18	Sum	=SUM(B12:E12,B14:E14)				
19	Buffer in %	8%				
20	Buffer in $					
21	Upper limit					
22						
23						

Advice: Previously, the functions usually only had one range in parentheses. This sum function contains two ranges. They are separated by a comma (,). A colon (:) in the range specification means *to*. The comma (,) stands for *and*. The formula therefore reads as follows: Form the sum of the ranges B12 to E12 and B14 to E14. This notation can also be transferred to other functions, e.g. MIN, MAX or AVERAGE. More than two ranges are also possible. You get the same result with the notation **=SUM(B12:E12)+SUM(B14:E14)**. As the first notation is shorter, you should prefer this.

11.3.15 Changing the percentage value

51. Select cell B19. The cell is already formatted with the format **Percentage**.

16		
17	Material and machines	
18	Sum	95,010,000
19	Buffer in %	8%
20	Buffer in $	
21	Upper limit	
22		

52. Enter the number **10** to change the value from 8 % to 10 %.

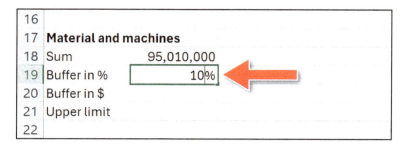

53. Confirm the entry using the **enter key** ⏎.

11.3.16 Calculating the buffer

54. Enter the formula **=B18*B19** in B20 to calculate the buffer in dollar.

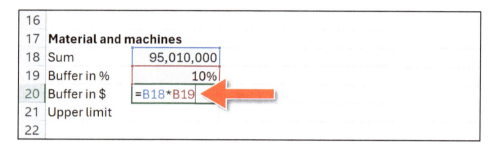

Advice: The content of B19 is the value 10 %. To calculate 10 % of B18, the two values must be multiplied. 10 % corresponds to 0.1. The values are mathematically equal.

55. Enter the formula **=B18+B20** in cell B21 to determine the upper limit.

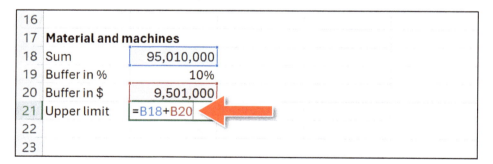

11.3.17 Conclusion

56. Save the file and close Excel.

12   Exercise: Business trip

This exercise serves as a learning check and is the conclusion of the second section. Unlike instructions, the solution is not described here. You can see an illustration of the finished table on the right side.

12.1   Contents

* correcting functions
* calculating with dates and percentages
* cell and text formats

12.2   Exercise

1. Open the sample file *Chapter 12 - Business trip - Start - B2* and enable editing.
2. Delete all formats in cell D4.
3. Delete the date and the date format in cell D8.
4. Calculate the number of overnight stays in cell B5. To do this, subtract the two dates.
5. Enter the net price **95** in cell B7.
    Advice: The net price is the price without sales tax.
6. Set the *dollar* format for cell B7.
7. Calculate the net price for the specified overnight stays in cell B8.
8. Enter the sales tax rate 8 % in cell B10.
9. Calculate the sales tax in dollar in cell B11.
10. Calculate the billing amount in cell B12.
    Advice: The billing amount is calculated by adding the net price and the sales tax. As the invoice amount includes sales tax, it is also referred to as the gross amount.
11. Save the file and close Excel.

	A	B
1	**Business trip**	
2		
3	Arrival	10/20/2023
4	Departure	10/26/2023
5	Overnight stays	6
6		
7	Net cost per day	$ 95.00
8	Net cost	$ 570.00
9		
10	Sales tax in %	8%
11	Sales tax in $	$ 45.60
12	Billing amount	$ 615.60
13		

Result: Business trip

Section 3

Instructions

Contents of this section:

- anchoring (fixing) cell references (dollar sign)
- frequent error messages

13   Instruction: Wages

Use this guide to calculate the wages for a company's employees.

13.1   New content

- fix (anchor) cell references
- error message #VALUE

13.2   Repetitions

- AutoSum button

13.3   Instruction

13.3.1   *Opening the sample file*

1. Open the sample file **Chapter 13 - Wages - Start - B2** and enable editing.

13.3.2   *Moving cells*

There is an error in the table. Cell A2 should be moved to A3.

2. Select cell A2. Point the mouse at the desired position on the green border of the cell pointer. However, do <u>not</u> point to the fill handle.

	A	B	C
1	Wages		
2			
3	**Hourly rate**	$ 20.00	
4			
5	Name	Hours	Wage
6	Jones	165	$ 3,300.00
7	Lopez	186	$ 3,720.00
8	Brown	201	$ 4,020.00
9	Williams	130	$ 2,600.00
10	Gomez	147	$ 2,940.00
11	Hill	195	$ 3,900.00
12	Wright	128	$ 2,560.00
13	Green	54	$ 1,080.00
14	Cruz	69	$ 1,380.00
15	Myers	174	$ 3,480.00
16		1449	$ 28,980.00
17			

Result: Wages

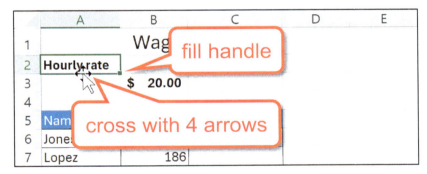

Result: The mouse pointer is displayed with a cross consisting of four arrows 🖰.
Advice: This mouse pointer symbolizes the moving of cells. The fill handle is only used to fill cells, not to move them.

3. Hold down the left mouse button and drag the mouse to cell A3. Pay attention to the green frame.

Advice: The thick green border symbolizes the new position of the cell.

4. Release the mouse button.

Result: Cell A2 is moved to A3. The formats are also maintained.

13.3.3   Determining the wages

In column C, the employees' wages are to be determined.

5. Enter the formula **=B6*B3** in cell C6.

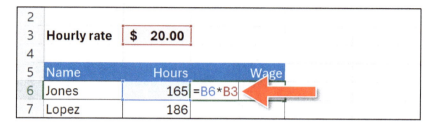

6. Look at the result.

5	Name	Hours	Wage
6	Jones	165	$ 3,300.00
7	Lopez	186	

13.3.4   Consciously making mistakes

The formula in cell C6 is completely correct. However, it has a decisive disadvantage. Incorrect results are produced when the formula is copied. To see this result, it makes sense to consciously make this mistake once. Bear this in mind for the next steps: When copying formulas vertically, the <u>numbers</u> of the cell references are changed

7. Select C6 and copy the formula with the fill handle to cells C7 to C14.
8. Look at the result.

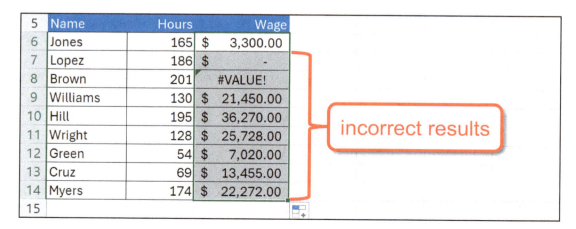

5	Name	Hours	Wage
6	Jones	165	$ 3,300.00
7	Lopez	186	$ -
8	Brown	201	#VALUE!
9	Williams	130	$ 21,450.00
10	Hill	195	$ 36,270.00
11	Wright	128	$ 25,728.00
12	Green	54	$ 7,020.00
13	Cruz	69	$ 13,455.00
14	Myers	174	$ 22,272.00
15			

Advice: The results in cells C7 to C14 are incorrect.

13.3.5   Checking the incorrect results

9. Select cell C7 and look at the formula bar.

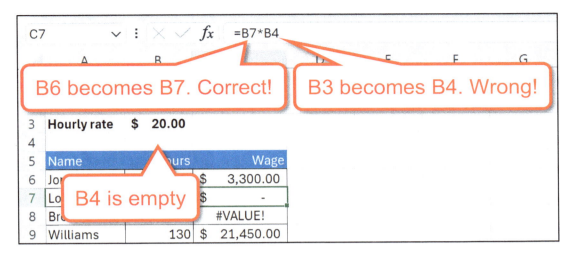

Advice: When filling formulas vertically, Excel changes the numbers of the cell references (the row number). This value is increased by 1 per row. However, Excel does not check whether the change makes sense! The original formula in C6 is: **=B6*B3**. By copying, the formula **=B7*B4** is entered in cell C7. Changing the cell reference from B6 to B7 is correct. Changing the cell reference from B3 to B4 is not intended. This reference should not have been changed. B4 is an empty cell. The formula therefore displays a dash in cell C7. The dash represents the value 0. Cell C8 displays the error message **#VALUE!** The formula in this cell is: **=B8*B5**. However, cell B5 does not contain a value (not a number), but a text. As it is not possible to calculate with text, Excel displays this error message.

13.3.6   Checking the formula with F2

10. Press the **function key** F2 while C7 is still selected to activate edit mode.

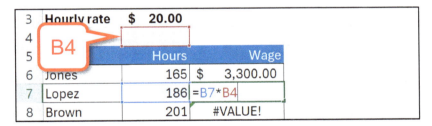

Advice: The active edit mode makes it easy to recognize the error. The colored highlighting of the cells shows that the reference to cell B4 is incorrect.

11. Press the **escape key** Esc to exit edit mode again.

   Or: As you have not made any changes to the cell, you can also press the **enter key** ↵ in this situation to exit the edit mode again.

13.3.7   Correcting the formula - anchoring cell references

12. Select C6 and press the **function key** F2 to enter edit mode.

13. Change the formula to **=B6*B$3** to anchor the reference to row 3. Pay attention to the dollar sign in front of the 3.

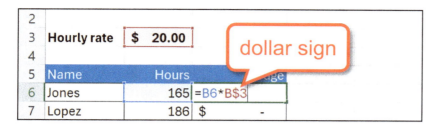

Advice: The dollar sign ($) in front of the 3 prevents the 3 from being changed when using the fill function. This notation is referred to as a **mixed reference** or **absolute reference**.
Read more: Please also read Chapter 25 Explanation: Cell references, page 144.

14. Confirm the entry. Select cell C6 and copy the formula to cells C7 to C14.

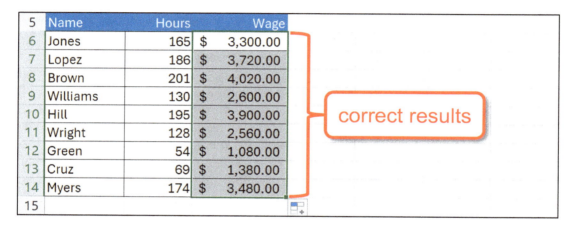

Advice: The old contents of the cells are overwritten when filling in the formula again.

13.3.8   Checking the formulas

15. Highlight C7 and press the **function key** F2 to activate the edit mode.

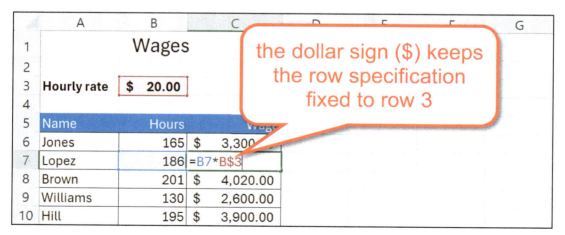

Advice: The cell reference B6 has been changed to B7. The reference B$3 has not been changed this time. The dollar sign ($) in front of the 3 prevents the row reference 3 from being changed.

---

16. Also check the formula in cell C8.

7	Lopez	186	$	3,720.00
8	Brown	201	=B8*B$3	
9	Williams	130	$	2,600.00

Advice: B7 has been changed to B8. B$3 remains unchanged.

13.3.9 AutoSum button

17. Select cells B6 to C15 and click on the **AutoSum** button $\boxed{\Sigma}$. However, do <u>not</u> click on the arrow $\boxed{\vee}$ next to the button.

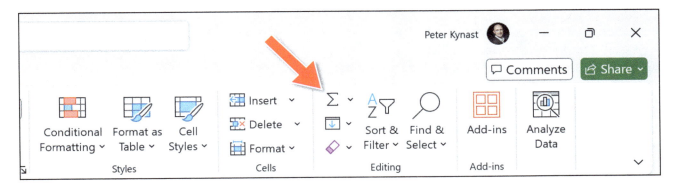

Result: The sums of the two columns are displayed in cells B15 in C15.

18. Select cell B15 and check the formula in the formula bar.

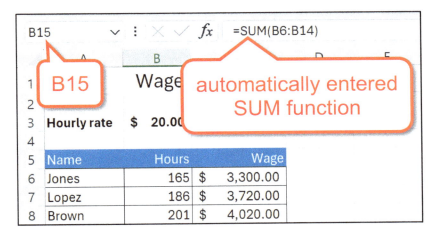

Advice: It is not important whether you enter the **SUM** function manually or use the **AutoSum** button. The two methods are equivalent.

19. Check the formula in C15 as well.

13.3.10 Inserting rows

20. Select any cell in row 10.

9	Williams	130	$	2,600.00	
10	Hill	195		0	
11	Wright	128	$	2,560.00	

21. Click on the arrow ⌄ next to the **Insert** button 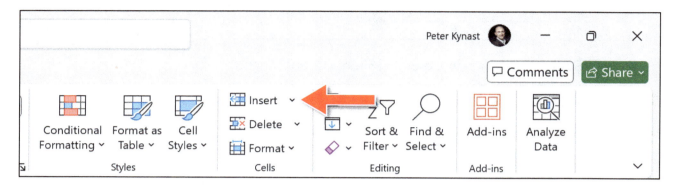 to open the list box for this button. Do not click on the icon or text of the button.

Advice: Clicking directly on the text or symbol would insert a single empty cell. The cells below would be moved down by one row.

22. Click on the **Insert Sheet Rows** list item to insert a new row.

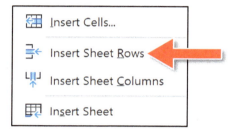

Result: A new row is inserted above row 10. It has the same formats as the adjacent rows. The functions in row 16 are automatically adapted to the enlarged table.

Advice: Rows are always inserted above the selected row. This means you can also insert a row above row 1. Columns are always inserted to the left of the selected column. In this way, you are able to insert a new column to the left of column A. The terms row and sheet row are synonymous. Sheet column and column also have the same meaning.

13.3.11 Checking the function

23. Select B16 and press the **function key** F2 to activate edit mode.

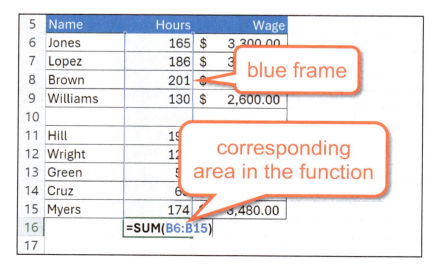

Or: Of course, you can also check the formula by looking at the formula bar. The advantage of activating edit mode is that the cell area of the function is highlighted by a blue frame. The corresponding area within the function has the same color.

13.3.12 Data entry

24. Exit edit mode by pressing the **enter key** ⏎ or the **escape key** Esc.

    Advice: You have not changed any data. It therefore makes no difference whether you exit the cell with enter or escape.

25. Enter the following data in row 10.

9	Williams		130	$	2,600.00
10	Gomez	147			
11	Hi		195	$	3,900.00
12	Wr nt		128	$	2,560.00
13	Gr n		54	$	1,080.00
14	Cruz		69	$	1,380.00

26. Confirm the entry and look at the result.

9	Williams	130	$	2,600.00
10	Gomez	147	$	2,940.00
11	Hill	195	$	3,900.00
12	Wright	128	$	2,560.00
13	Green	54	$	1,080.00
14	Cruz	69	$	1,380.00

C10 is calculated automatically

Result: When the entry in B10 is confirmed, the formula is automatically entered in C10. Excel recognizes the pattern and the formulas it contains.

27. Select C10 and press the **function key** F2 to activate edit mode to check the formula in C10.

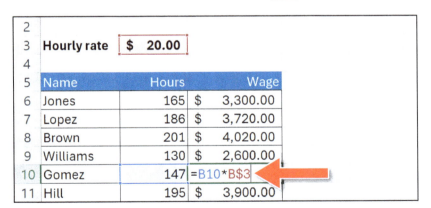

Advice: The colored highlighting of the cells and the corresponding cell references makes it easy to check. The automatically entered formula is correct. However, do not blindly rely on Excel's automatic functions. Be sure to carry out checks. Only when you can reliably predict the effect of an automatic function should you reduce the number of checks.

13.3.13 Conclusion

28. Save the file and close Excel.

14   Instruction: Commissions

Use this guide to calculate commission payments for several branches of a company.

14.1   New content

- inserting several columns at the same time
- selecting related areas quickly

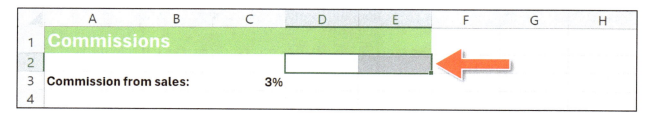

	A	B	C	D	E	F	G	H
1	**Commissions**							
2								
3	Commission from sales:		3%					
4								
5	**Branch**	**Anaheim**	**Baltimore**	**Frisco**	**New York**	**Orlando**	**Seattle**	**Sums**
6	Sales volume	501571	625871	175614	201320	458720	320145	2283241
7	Commission	15047.13	18776.13	5268.42	6039.6	13761.6	9604.35	68497.23
8								

Result: Commissions

14.2   Repetitions

- anchoring cell references
- AutoSum button

14.3   Instruction

14.3.1   Opening the sample file

1. Open the sample file **Chapter 14 - Commissions - Start - B2** and enable editing.

14.3.2   Inserting multiple columns

The number of columns inserted matches the number of columns currently selected. In the next step, two columns are to be inserted before column D.

2. Select the cells D2 to E2.

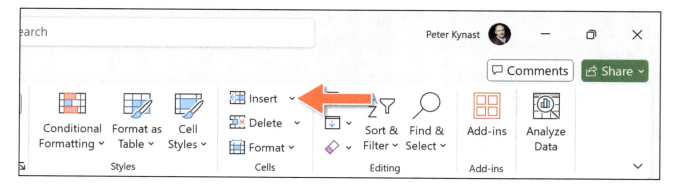

Advice: The row number or the number of rows are not decisive. You could also have selected D5 to E5 or D6 to E20. It is also possible to select the entire columns D and E.

3. Click on the arrow ⌄ next to the **Insert** button [Insert ⌄] to open the list box for this button.

4. Click on the **Insert Sheet Columns** list item.

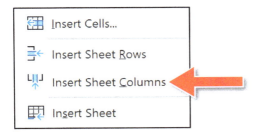

> **Result:** Two new columns are inserted on the left before column D. They receive the formats of the adjacent columns.
> **Advice:** The terms columns and sheet columns are synonymous.

14.3.3 Data entry

5. Enter the following data in cells D5 to E6.

	Branch	Anaheim	Baltimore	Frisco	New York	Orlando	Seattle
4							
5	Branch	Anaheim	Baltimore	Frisco	New York	Orlando	Seattle
6	Sales volume	501571	625871	175614	201320	458720	320145
7	Commission						
8							

14.3.4 Determining the commissions

When calculating the commissions, another common error is deliberately shown in following steps.

6. Enter the formula **=B6*C3** in cell B7.
   Advice: Cell references can be entered manually or using the pointing method. With the pointing method, you have the choice between clicking on the cell(s) or selecting with the arrow keys (cursor keys). Decide which input method is better for you.
7. Look at the result.

	Branch	Anaheim	Baltimore	Frisco	New York	Orlando	Seattle
5	Branch	Anaheim	Baltimore	Frisco	New York	Orlando	Seattle
6	Sales volume	501571	625871	175614	201320	458720	320145
7	Commission	15047.13					
8							
9							

Advice: The formula in cell B7 is completely correct. However, it has a decisive disadvantage. Copying the formula produces incorrect results. To see the result, it makes sense to consciously make this mistake once. Bear this in mind for the next steps: When copying formulas horizontally, the letters (column references) in the cell references are automatically changed.

8. Copy the formula from B7 to cells C7 to G7 using the fill handle.
9. Look at the result. Incorrect results are displayed.

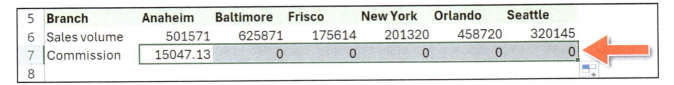

	Branch	Anaheim	Baltimore	Frisco	New York	Orlando	Seattle
5	Branch	Anaheim	Baltimore	Frisco	New York	Orlando	Seattle
6	Sales volume	501571	625871	175614	201320	458720	320145
7	Commission	15047.13	0	0	0	0	0
8							

14.3.5   Checking the incorrect results

10. Select C7 and press the **function key** F2 to activate edit mode.

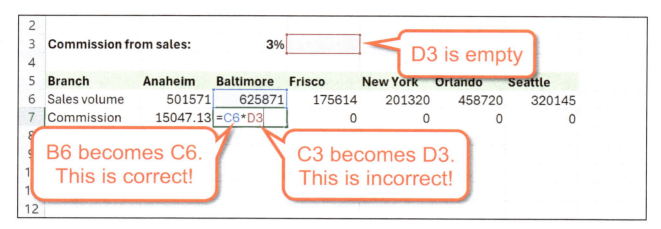

Result: The letters of the cell references are changed by copying. They are advanced by one letter in the alphabet per column. B6 becomes C6 and C3 becomes D3. However, the second change should not have been made. To prevent this, column C in cell B7 must be set with a dollar sign ($).

11. Press the **enter key** ↵ or the **escape key** Esc to exit edit mode.

     Advice: As you have not changed the content of the cell, there is no difference between these two keys in this situation.

14.3.6   Correcting the formula

12. Correct the formula in cell B7 to **=B6*$C3**.

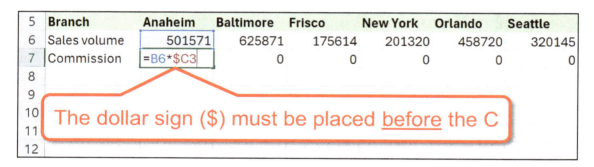

     Advice: The dollar sign ($) must be placed before the letter C. This fixes the reference to column C.

13. Copy the corrected formula to the cells C7 to G7 again to overwrite the incorrect formulas.

14.3.7   AutoSum button

14. Select the cells B6 to H7.

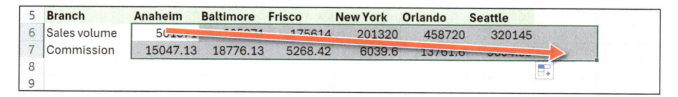

     Advice: There are various ways to select the area for the AutoSum. In some cases, however, this can lead to undesirable results. If you select the values and the corresponding result cells (B6 to H7) as described in the instructions, no errors can occur when calculating sums.

15. Click on the **AutoSum** button $\boxed{\Sigma}$ to calculate the sums of the selected rows.

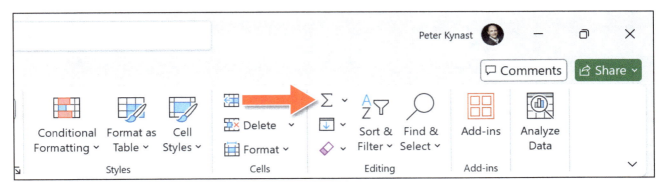

16. Look at the result.

5	Branch	Anaheim	Baltimore	Frisco	New York	Orlando	Seattle	
6	Sales volume	501571	625871	175614	201320	458720	320145	2283241
7	Commission	15047.13	18776.13	5268.42	6039.6	13761.6	9604.35	68497.23
8								

Result: Excel inserts the sums into the empty cells (H6 and H7).

17. Enter the heading **Sum** in cell H5 and look at the result.

4								
5	Branch	Anaheim	Baltimore	Frisco	New York	Orlando	Seattle	Sum
6	Sales volume	501571	625871	175614	201320	458720	320145	2283241

Result: The formats have already been used three times in the adjacent cells on the left. They are therefore automatically adopted for H5 when the input is confirmed.

14.3.8   Copying formats

Filling cells with the black cross is usually used to copy the contents and formats of a cell to other cells, e.g. formulas, text or numbers. You can also use the black cross to copy just the formats to other cells.

18. Select the cell G1.
19. Point to the fill handle and while holding down the left mouse button, drag the mouse to cell H1 to copy the format.

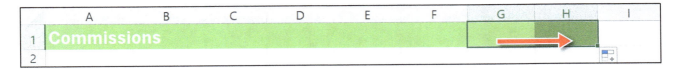

Result: The format of cell G1 (fill color) is copied to H1.

14.3.9   Creating colored borders.

20. Select any cell in the area A5 to H7.

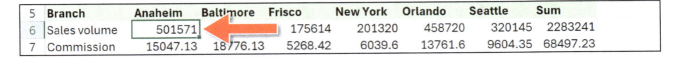

21. Press the keyboard shortcut **control key** Ctrl + A (**select all**) to select the related area.

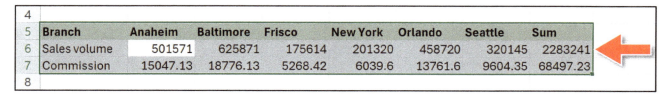

	Branch	Anaheim	Baltimore	Frisco	New York	Orlando	Seattle	Sum
4								
5	Branch	Anaheim	Baltimore	Frisco	New York	Orlando	Seattle	Sum
6	Sales volume	501571	625871	175614	201320	458720	320145	2283241
7	Commission	15047.13	18776.13	5268.42	6039.6	13761.6	9604.35	68497.23
8								

Advice: The **select all** command is misleading. The entire worksheet is not selected. The cells that are recognized as a related area are selected. Using **select all** twice would select the entire sheet.

22. Click on the arrow ⌄ next to the **Borders** button ⊞ ⌄ to open the list box for this button.

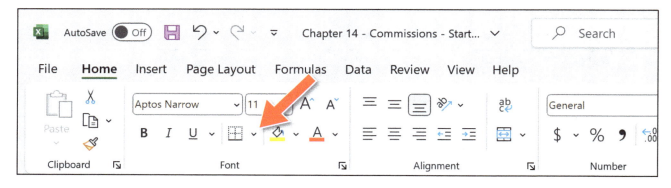

23. Click on the **More Borders** list item at the bottom of the list box.

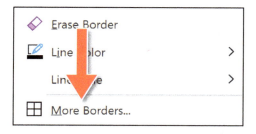

Result: The **Format Cells** dialog box opens. The **Border** tab is active.

24. Click on the small arrow ⌄ next to the **Color** list box to open the list box.

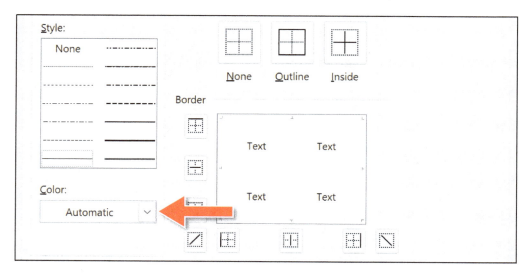

25. In the color palette, click on the button for the color **Green, Accent 6, Darker 25%**.

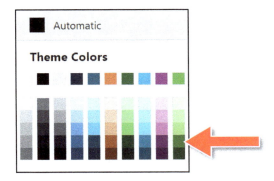

> **Advice:** If borders of a different color are to be formatted, the color must be selected first. The actual border settings can then be assigned in the newly selected color.

26. Click on the **Outline** button 🔲 and the **Inside** button 🔲 to add outer and inner borders to the selected area. Pay attention to the preview.

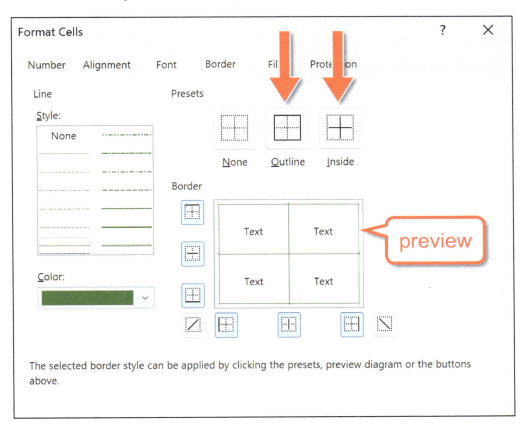

> **Advice:** Also pay attention to the colors of the borders in the preview. Only if the borders are displayed in color here will they also be displayed in color in the table.

27. Click on the **OK** button to confirm the settings.

14.3.10 Conclusion

28. Save the file and close Excel.

15   Instruction: Hardware store

Use this guide to create a calculation for the product categories of a hardware store.

15.1   New content

- error message #DIV/0!

15.2   Repetitions

- anchoring (fixing) cell references

15.3   Instruction

15.3.1   Opening the sample file

1. Open the sample file **Chapter 15 - Hardware store - Start - B2** and enable editing.

15.3.2   Determining percentages

Column C will be used to determine the percentage shares of the product categories of the total sales. Two errors are deliberately shown in the beginning for demonstration purposes.

	A	B	C
1	**Hardware store**		
2	Revenue percentages		
3			
4	**Product category**	**Revenue**	**Percentage**
5	Paint	$ 115,395.00	5.0%
6	Construction material	$ 470,416.00	20.4%
7	Household hardware	$ 394,061.00	17.1%
8	Electronics	$ 469,594.00	20.4%
9	Tools	$ 312,522.00	13.6%
10	Garden	$ 236,253.00	10.3%
11	Bathroom	$ 294,473.00	12.8%
12	Sweets	$ 11,025.00	0.5%
13	**Total**	**$ 2,303,739.00**	
14			

Result: Hardware store

2. Enter the formula **=B5/B12*100** in cell C5 to determine the percentage share of colors of the total sales.

4	**Product category**	**Revenue**	**Percentage**	
5	Paint	$ 115,395.00	=B5/B12*100	⬅
6	Construction material	$ 470,416.00		

Advice: Mathematically, this formula is correct. However, it cannot be copied to the other cells without errors. Copying the formula to the cells below will make this error visible.

3. Copy the formula to cells C6 to C11 and look at the result.

4	**Product category**	**Revenue**	**Percentage**
5	Paint	$ 115,395.00	5.03311796
6	Construction material	$ 470,416.00	#DIV/0!
7	Household hardware	$ 394,061.00	#DIV/0!
8	Electronics	$ 469,594.00	#DIV/0!
9	Tools	$ 312,522.00	#DIV/0!
10	Garden	$ 236,253.00	#DIV/0!
11	Bathroom	$ 294,473.00	#DIV/0!
12	**Total**	**$ 2,292,714.00**	

error message because the cell is divided by zero

Result: The error message **#DIV/0!** is displayed in the filled cells.

Advice: The message appears because a division with zero is being carried out. Dividing by zero is not mathematically possible. This error is therefore displayed.

15.3.3   Checking the incorrect formulas

4.   Select C6 and press the **function key** $\boxed{F2}$ to activate edit mode.

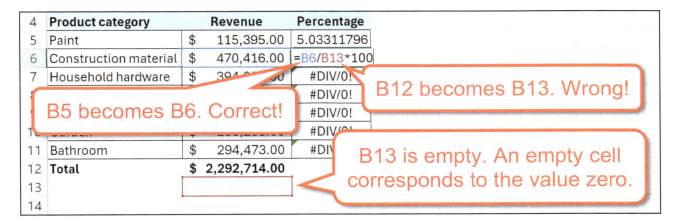

Advice: When filling cells vertically, Excel changes the <u>numbers</u> of the cell references. As a result, the reference was changed from B5 to B6. This change is desired. The change from B12 to B13 is not desired. B13 is an empty cell. An empty cell corresponds to the value zero. B6 is therefore divided by zero. Division by zero is not mathematically possible.

15.3.4   Partial correction of the formula

The following formula is mathematically correct and can be copied. However, it is not yet finished. When using the percentage format, you will encounter a new problem.

5.   Change the formula in cell C5 to **=B5/B$12*100**.

4	Product category		Revenue	Percentage
5	Paint	$	115,395.00	=B5/B$12*100
6	Construction material	$	470,416.00	#DIV/0!
7	Household hardware	$	394,061.00	#DIV/0!

Advice: The 12 must not be changed when copied. The dollar sign must therefore be placed <u>in front of</u> the 12.

6.   Copy the formula from C5 to cells C6 to C11.

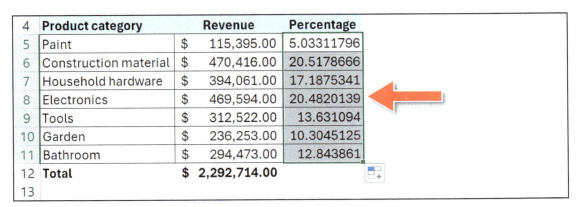

4	Product category		Revenue	Percentage
5	Paint	$	115,395.00	5.03311796
6	Construction material	$	470,416.00	20.5178666
7	Household hardware	$	394,061.00	17.1875341
8	Electronics	$	469,594.00	20.4820139
9	Tools	$	312,522.00	13.631094
10	Garden	$	236,253.00	10.3045125
11	Bathroom	$	294,473.00	12.843861
12	Total	$	2,292,714.00	
13				

Result: The correct results are displayed. However, they are displayed without a percentage sign. The old formulas are overwritten when they are filled in again.

7. Format C5 to C11 with the format **Percentage** % and look at the result.

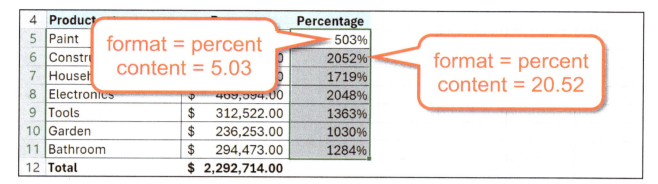

Result: The values are displayed in the **Percentage** format.

Advice: When assigning the percentage format, the percentage value that corresponds to the content of the cell is displayed! The content of cell C5 is 5.03. This value corresponds to the percentage value 503%. The same principle applies to the following cells.

Read more: Please also read Chapter 24 Explanation: Contents and formats, page 143.

15.3.5 Correcting the formula

The calculations are mathematically correct. However, due to the percentage format, the percentages displayed are 100 times too large. As a solution, the factor 100 is removed from the formula.

8. Correct the formula in C5 to **=B5/B$12** and copy the formula to the cells below.

4	Product category	Revenue		Percentage
5	Paint	$	115,395.00	5%
6	Construction material	$	470,416.00	21%
7	Household hardware	$	394,061.00	17%
8	Electronics	$	469,594.00	20%

correct results

15.3.6 Adding a decimal place

9. Check whether the cell range C5 to C11 is still selected.

10. Click on the **Increase Decimal** button ←0 .00 to display percentage values with a single decimal place.

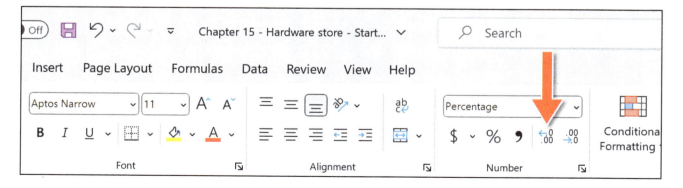

Advice: Excel does not always display all decimal places. However, all decimal places are considered when calculating. It is not important whether they are visible!

15.3.7   Inserting a row

11. Click on the row header of row 12 and then click on the **Insert** button 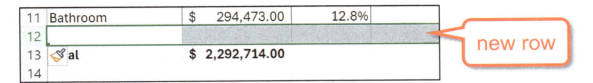 to insert a new row above row 12.

11	Bathroom	$ 294,473.00	12.8%	new row
12				
13	al	$ 2,292,714.00		
14				

12. Check the cell range in cell B13. It currently reads: **B5:B11**

11	Bathroom	$ 294,473.00	12.8%
12			
13	Total	=SUM(B5:B11)	
14			

> **Advice:** This check makes it clearer what will happen in the next step. B12 is not part of the range specification at this point.

15.3.8   Data entry

13. Enter the word **Sweets** in A12 and the revenue figure **11025** in B12. Look at the result.

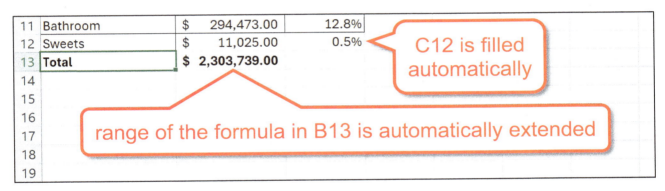

11	Bathroom	$ 294,473.00	12.8%
12	Sweets	$ 11,025.00	0.5%
13	Total	$ 2,303,739.00	
14			

C12 is filled automatically

range of the formula in B13 is automatically extended

> **Result:** When the entry in cell B12 is completed, the formula is automatically entered in C12. At the same time, the cell range in cell B13 is enlarged. It is now B5 to B12. The new value in cell B12 is included.

14. Press the **function key** [F2] to check the cell range in cell B13.

12	Sweets	$ 11,025.00	0.5%
13	Total	=SUM(B5:B12)	
14			

> **Advice:** Excel's automatic corrections are versatile. However, do not rely on them blindly. You should always carry out checks for new processes. Only when you have gained sufficient experience with automatic corrections should you spend less time with checks.

15. Format the cells A12 to C12 with **All Borders**.

15.3.9   Conclusion

16. Save the file and close Excel.

16 Instruction: Election results

Use these instructions to calculate the percentage of votes in the 2022 United States Senate election in Vermont.

16.1 New content

- Anchoring cell references using the function key F4

Result: Election results

16.2 Repetitions

- Anchoring (fixing) cell references
- increase decimal

16.3 Instruction

16.3.1 Opening the sample file

1. Open the sample file **Chapter 16 - Election results - Start - B2** and enable editing.

16.3.2 Determining percentages

2. Enter the formula **=B5/J5** in cell B6 to calculate the percentage values. However, do not complete the entry yet.

Advice: The formula should then be copied to cells C6 to J6. You already know that the formula is incomplete. To ensure that the reference to column J is not changed, a dollar sign ($) must be placed in front of it. Below you can see another option for inserting the dollar sign.

3. Press the **function key** F4 to change the reference and insert dollar signs.

Result: The cell reference J5 is changed. A dollar sign is inserted before the J and before the 5.
Advice: This reference would also lead to the correct result. However, the dollar sign in front of the 5 has no effect.
Attention: If you are working on a laptop or with a smaller keyboard, you sometimes have to use the key combination **Fn key** Fn + F4 to activate the **function key** F4.
Read more: Please also read Chapter 26 Explanation: Keyboard shortcuts, page 146.

4. Press the **function key** $\boxed{\text{F4}}$ again.

4	**Candidate**	**Peter Welch**	**Gerald Malloy**	**Dawn Ellis**	**Kerry Raheb**
5	Votes	196,575	80,468	2,752	1,532
6	Percentage	=B5/J$5			
7					

Result: The cell reference is changed again. Currently there is only a dollar sign in front of the 5.
Advice: This notation would not lead to the correct result. The formula will be copied horizontally. The dollar sign must therefore be written <u>before</u> the letter J. A dollar sign <u>in front of</u> the number has no effect when copying horizontally.

5. Press the **function key** $\boxed{\text{F4}}$ again.

4	**Candidate**	**Peter Welch**	**Gerald Malloy**	**Dawn Ellis**	**Kerry Raheb**
5	Votes	196,575	80,468	2,752	1,532
6	Percentage	=B5/$J5			
7					

Result: The cell reference is changed again. The dollar sign is now in the correct position in front of the letter J.
Advice: Whether you type in the dollar signs manually or use the function key $\boxed{\text{F4}}$ is a matter of preference.

6. Confirm the entry. Copy the formula to cells C6 to J6.

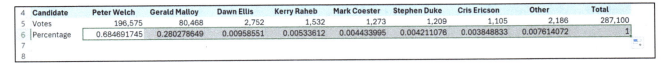

4	Candidate	Peter Welch	Gerald Malloy	Dawn Ellis	Kerry Raheb	Mark Coester	Stephen Duke	Cris Ericson	Other	Total
5	Votes	196,575	80,468	2,752	1,532	1,273	1,209	1,105	2,186	287,100
6	Percentage	0.684691745	0.280278649	0.00958551	0.00533612	0.004433995	0.004211076	0.003848833	0.007614072	1
7										
8										

Advice: In mathematics, the factor 100 is used to calculate percentages. As the percentage format is then assigned, the factor 100 is omitted in this formula. In Excel, the percentage format replaces the factor 100.

16.3.3 Percentage format

7. Format the cells B6 to J6 with the number format **Percentage** $\boxed{\%}$.

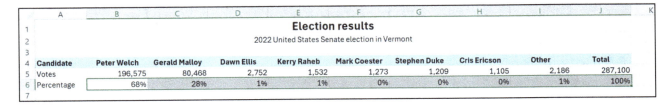

Result: The numbers are displayed in percentage format without decimal places. The percentage values that correspond to the content of the cells are displayed.
Examples: 0.329 corresponds to 32.9 %, 0.205 corresponds to 20.5 % and 0.126 corresponds to 12.6 %.

16.3.4 Increasing decimal places

8. Check whether the cell range B6 to J6 is still selected.

9. Click on the **Increase Decimal** button to display a decimal place for the selected numbers.

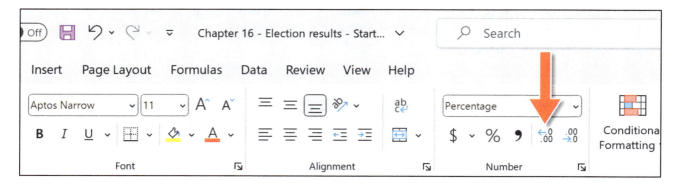

Advice: All decimal places are always considered when calculating in Excel. It is not important whether the decimal places are visible or not.

10. Look at the result.

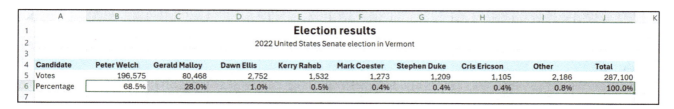

16.3.5 Adding border formatting

11. Press the key combination **control key** Ctrl + A to select the contiguous table area A4 to J6.

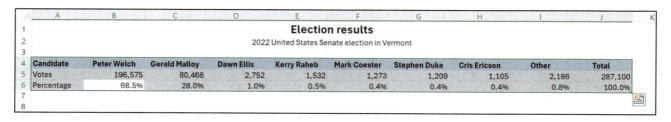

Advice: The keyboard shortcut **control key** Ctrl + A activates the **select all** command. Excel selects the area that is recognized as related. Pressing this keyboard shortcut again will select the entire worksheet.

12. Format this area with **All Borders** ⊞.

16.3.6 Conclusion

13. Save the file and close Excel.

Deviations

Work through this book at least once without deviating from the instructions. When working through it a second time, feel free to integrate your own changes.

17   Exercise: Paper consumption

This exercise serves as a learning check and is the conclusion of the third section. Unlike instructions, the solution is not described here. You can see an illustration of the finished table on the right side.

17.1   Contents

- functions: SUM, MIN, MAX, AVERAGE
- anchoring cell references
- calculating percentages
- Auto Fill Options

17.2   Exercise

1. Open the sample file **Chapter 17 - Paper consumption - Start - B2** and enable editing.
2. Calculate the total consumption of paper reams in cell B14.
3. Calculate the average, the highest value and the lowest value in cells B15, B16 and B17.
4. In cell C5, calculate the percentage share of the 1st Ave of the total consumption in B14. To do this, divide the value from cell B5 by the total consumption in B14. The formula should then be copied to the cells below. The row number of the of the total consumption must not change when copying the formula.
5. Copy the formula to cells C6 to C17. Only copy the formula and not the formats. The original colors should be retained.
6. Set the format **Percentage** for cells C5 to C17 with one decimal place.
7. Save the file and close Excel.

	A	B	C
1	**Paper consumption**		
2	March 2024		
3			
4	**Branch**	**Reams**	**Percentage**
5	1st Ave	89	12.0%
6	Academy St	139	18.7%
7	Dover St	121	16.3%
8	Grand St	127	17.1%
9	Madison Ave	90	12.1%
10	River Rd	48	6.5%
11	Spring St	54	7.3%
12	The Mall	32	4.3%
13	Wheeler Ave	44	5.9%
14	Sum	744	100.0%
15	Average	83	11.1%
16	Highest value	139	18.7%
17	Lowest value	32	4.3%
18			

Result: Paper consumption

Dear reader,

ityco is a small company. Please consider supporting us by reviewing this book on Amazon.

With kind regards, Peter Kynast ❤

You can submit your review in your Amazon orders with a single click. Even if you did not buy the book yourself, you can still leave a review. Search "Peter Kynast" on Amazon and click on "Write a costumer review" on the product page. You can also scan this QR-Code, it will take you to the review page.

Section 4

Instructions

Contents of this section:

- linking cells
- adding times
- custom date formats
- adding numbers quickly
- sorting data

18   Instruction: Work hours

Use these instructions to sum up monthly work hours.

18.1   New content

- linking cells
- number formatting codes
- adding times
- quick addition with the status bar

18.2   Repetitions

- filling several cells at once
- adjusting column width to a specific cell

18.3   Instruction

18.3.1   Opening the sample file

1.   Open the sample file **Chapter 18 - Work hours - Start - B2** and enable editing.

18.3.2   Simplifying date entries

Dates can be entered in full using the numeric keypad. This method is faster and simpler.

2.   Enter **10/1/23** in A4. Use the **forward slash** key /
     on the numeric keypad.

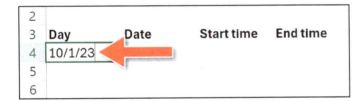

3.   Confirm the entry using the **enter key** ↵ on the numeric keypad and look at the result.

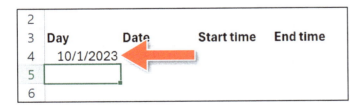

Result: The input is automatically converted into the date format. It is displayed in the standard no-tation **10/1/2023**.

Advice: Entering the date using the numeric keypad is faster and easier. You need to type fewer characters than in the **1/10/2023** notation. Your also have shorter input paths than using the top row of numbers. The numeric keypad is also referred to as numpad.

	Day	Date	Start time	End time	Break	Work hours
1	**Work hours**					
2						
3	**Day**	**Date**	**Start time**	**End time**	**Break**	**Work hours**
4	Sun	10/1/2023				
5	Mon	10/2/2023	8:00	16:00	1:00	7:00
6	Tue	10/3/2023	8:00	17:30	1:00	8:30
7	Wed	10/4/2023	8:00	18:21	1:00	9:21
8	Thu	10/5/2023	8:00	16:00	1:00	7:00
9	Fri	10/6/2023	8:00	16:00	1:00	7:00
10	Sat	10/7/2023				
11	Sun	10/8/2023				
12	Mon	10/9/2023	8:00	16:30	1:00	7:30
13	Tue	10/10/2023	8:00	16:00	1:00	7:00
14	Wed	10/11/2023	8:00	14:37	1:00	5:37
15	Thu	10/12/2023	8:00	19:08	1:00	10:08
16	Fri	10/13/2023	8:00	16:00	1:00	7:00
17	Sat	10/14/2023				
18	Sun	10/15/2023				
19	Mon	10/16/2023	8:00	15:30	1:00	6:30
20	Tue	10/17/2023	8:00	16:06	1:00	7:06
21	Wed	10/18/2023	8:00	16:00	1:00	7:00
22	Thu	10/19/2023	8:00	16:00	1:00	7:00
23	Fri	10/20/2023	8:00	17:15	1:00	8:15
24	Sat	10/21/2023				
25	Sun	10/22/2023				
26	Mon	10/23/2023	8:00	18:15	1:00	9:15
27	Tue	10/24/2023	8:00	16:00	1:00	7:00
28	Wed	10/25/2023	8:00	19:00	1:00	10:00
29	Thu	10/26/2023	8:00	16:00	1:00	7:00
30	Fri	10/27/2023	8:00	20:00	1:00	11:00
31	Sat	10/28/2023				
32	Sun	10/29/2023				
33	Mon	10/30/2023	8:00	16:00	1:00	7:00
34	Tue	10/31/2023	8:00	16:00	1:00	7:00
35	**Sum**					170:12:00
36						

Result: Work hours

4. Select cell A4 and point to the fill handle with the mouse.

5. Hold down the left mouse button and drag the mouse to row 34.

Result: The dates up to 10/31/2023 are entered in the cells. When filling cells, the current value is always displayed in the **tooltip**.

Advice: Dates are automatically incremented when copying. By pressing the **control key** `Ctrl` at the same time, you can stop the incrementing. The date is then duplicated.

18.3.3 Linking cells

Linking cells is very useful in many cases. You can carry over the content of a cell to another using a cell reference.

6. Enter the formula **=A4** in cell B4.

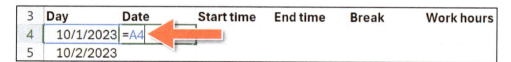

Advice: The quickest way to enter the cell reference is by pressing the **left arrow** key `←` after the equal sign (=) (pointing method). The cell reference is inserted automatically.

7. Confirm the entry and look at the result.

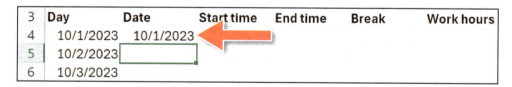

Result: The date is duplicated from A4 to cell B4. If A4 is changed, B4 would automatically adopt this change.

18.3.4 Copy cell links automatically

8. Select cell B4 and point to the fill handle with the mouse.

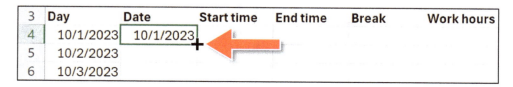

9. <u>Double-click</u> on the fill handle to automatically copy the formula to the cells below. Look at the result.

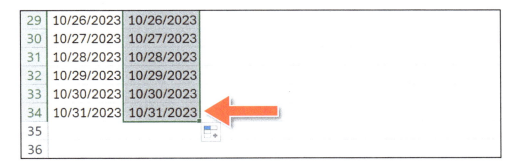

   Result: The formula is automatically copied up to the end of the table.

10. Select cell B5 and press the **function key** F2 to check the formula.

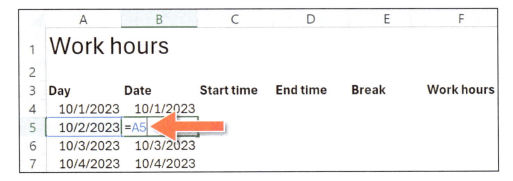

   Result: The cell reference has been automatically adjusted. It is linked to the content of cell A5.

11. Press the **enter key** ↵ or the **escape key** Esc to exit the edit mode.

18.3.5 Displaying dates as weekdays

The dates in column A should be displayed as 3-digit weekdays. To do this, a custom number format has to be created.

12. Select the cells A4 to A34. Click on the small arrow ⤡ at the bottom right of the **Number** group to open the **Format Cells** dialog box.

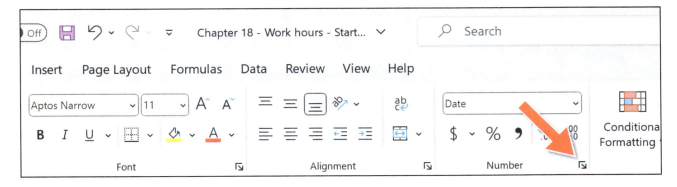

13. In the **Format Cells** dialog box, click on the **Custom** category.

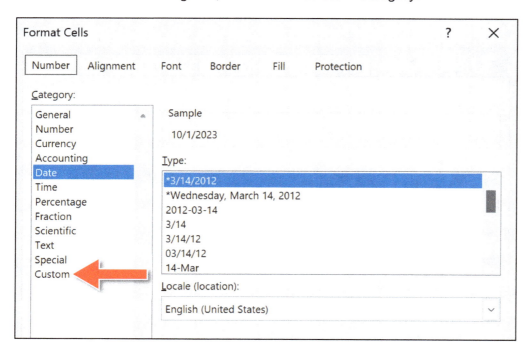

Advice: You can create your own number formats in this category.

14. Look at the settings in this category.

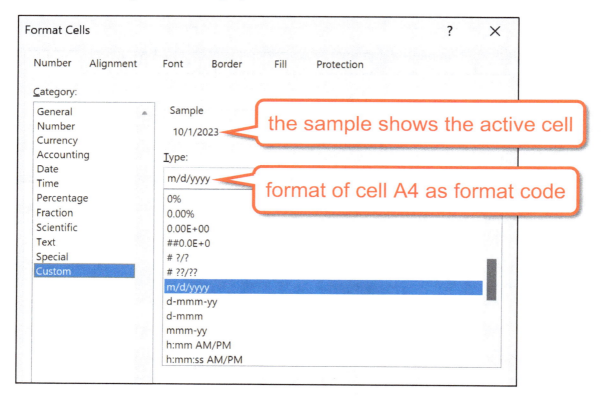

Advice: The example always refers to the active cell (currently A4). The active cell is easily recognizable in a selection. It is transparent so that the background color is visible. The date display 10/1/2023 is based on the format code **m/d/yyyy** (m = month, d = day, y = year). This format code can be changed and adapted in various ways.

15. Click in the *Type* field and delete the entire content. Pay attention to the sample shown.

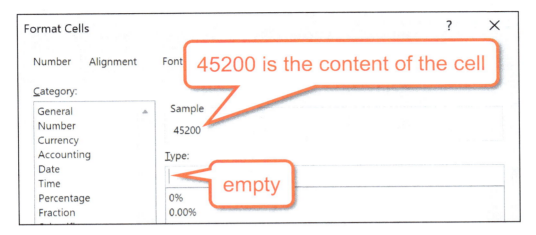

Result: The number 45200 is displayed in the sample.

Advice: Deleting the format code removes the format. The unformatted number in the cell becomes visible. 10/1/2023 is the 45200th day since 1/1/1900.

18.3.6   Entering the format code

16. Enter the letter *d* in the *Type* field. Pay attention to the sample again.

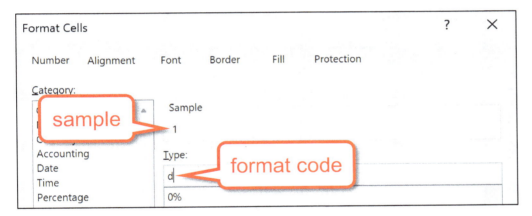

Result: The sample shows the value *1*.

Advice: The format code *d* (day) displays the day of the month as a single digit number. The display refers to the active cell A4. It contains the date 10/1/2023.

17. Enter another *d*.

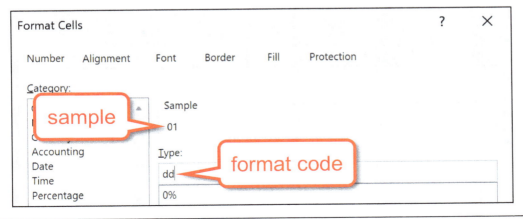

Result: The sample shows the value **01**.

Advice: The format code **dd** shows the day of the month as a 2-digit number. Numbers below 10 will receive a leading zero (1 = 01).

18. Enter another **d**.

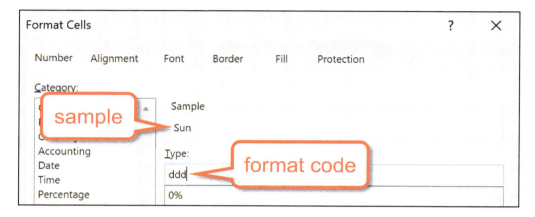

Result: The sample shows the abbreviation **Sun**.

Advice: The format code **ddd** displays the day as a 3-letter abbreviation. 10/1/2023 was a Sunday. The format code **dddd** would display the full name of the day **Sunday**.

19. Click on the **OK** button to accept the format.

Result: The dates are displayed as 3-letter abbreviations of the weekdays.

20. Look at the result.

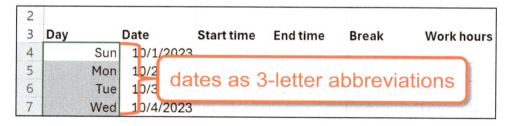

18.3.7   Adjusting the column width to a specific cell

The width of column A should be adjusted to the abbreviation **Wed**. However, double-clicking on the dividing line between column headers A and B would adjust the width to the longest content in the column (Work hours in A1).

21. Select cell A7 and click on the **Format** button to open the list box of the button.

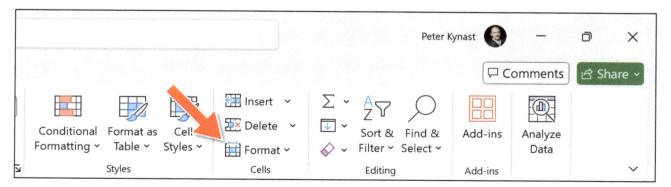

22. Click on the **AutoFit Column Width** list item to adjust the column width to the abbreviation **Wed**.

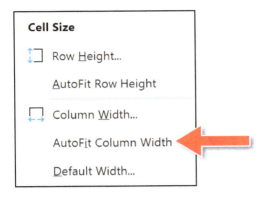

23. Look at the Result.

Result: The width of column A is adjusted to the abbreviation Wed.
Advice: To adjust the column width to specific content, the cell must be selected. Then select the **AutoFit Column Width** command.

24. Select Cells A4 to A34 and set the alignment to **Align Left** ▤ .

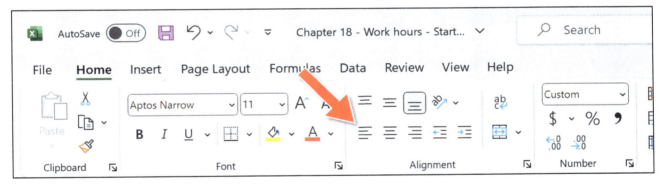

Advice: The contents of cells A4 to A34 are dates. Each date is a number! They are therefore displayed with right alignment in the beginning.

18.3.8 Filling several cells at the same time

The start of work in this company is 08:00. This time is entered first for all days. The weekends are deleted later.

25. Select the cells C4 to C34.

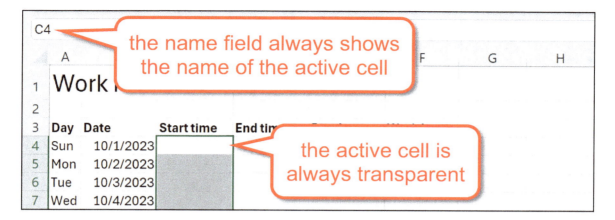

Advice: One cell is always active, even if several cells are selected. In this situation, cell C4 is the active cell. For this reason, C4 is the only cell in the selection that is not grayed out. The active cell is always transparent. The background color shines thorough unchanged.

26. Enter the time **08:00**. However, do not complete the entry yet.

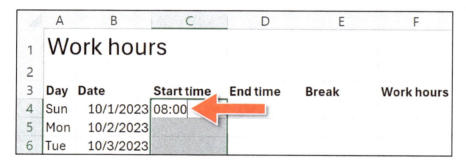

Advice: C4 is the active cell, so the entry is made in this cell. Times are entered with colons.
Attention: Do <u>not</u> add AM or PM to the times. The 24-hour time format is used this time.

27. Press and hold the **control key** | Ctrl | .

28. Press the **enter key** | ↵ | to complete the entry.

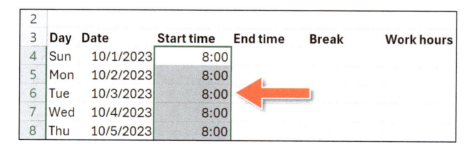

Result: The time is copied to all selected cells.

29. Release the **control key** | Ctrl | .

18.3.9   Opening the intermediate sample file

You need the end times to calculate the work hours. The file with these times is already prepared so that you do not have to enter them manually.

30. Save the file and close Excel.

31. Open the sample file ***Chapter 18 - Work hours - Intermediate result - B2*** and enable editing.

18.3.10 Entering breaks

32. Select the cells E4 to E34.

3	Day	Date	Start time	End time	Break	Work hours
4	Sun	10/1/2023	8:00	16:00		
5	Mon	10/2/2023	8:00	16:00		
6	Tue	10/3/2023	8:00	17:30		
7	Wed	10/4/2023	8:00	18:21		

active cell

33. Enter the time ***1:00***. However, do not complete the entry yet.

3	Day	Date	Start time	End time	Break	Work hours
4	Sun	10/1/2023	8:00	16:00	1:00	
5	Mon	10/2/2023	8:00	16:00		
6	Tue	10/3/2023	8:00	17:30		

   Advice: E4 is the active cell, so the entry is made in this cell.

34. Press and hold the ***control key*** | Ctrl |.

35. Press the ***enter key*** | ↵ | to complete the entry.

3	Day	Date	Start time	End time	Break	Work hours
4	Sun	10/1/2023	8:00	16:00	1:00	
5	Mon	10/2/2023	8:00	16:00	1:00	
6	Tue	10/3/2023	8:00	17:30	1:00	
7	Wed	10/4/2023	8:00	18:21	1:00	
8	Thu	10/5/2023	8:00	16:00	1:00	

automatically entered

   Result: The time entry is copied to all selected cells.

36. Release the ***control key*** | Ctrl | again.

18.3.11 Calculating work hours

37. Enter the formula ***=D4-C4-E4*** in cell F4 to calculate the work time.

3	Day	Date	Start time	End time	Break	Work hours
4	Sun	10/1/2023	8:00	16:00	1:00	=D4-C4-E4
5	Mon	10/2/2023	8:00	16:00	1:00	
6	Tue	10/3/2023	8:00	17:30	1:00	

   Advice: The start time (C4) and the break time (E4) are subtracted from the end time (D4).

38. Confirm the entry and select cell F4 again

39. Point to the fill handle with the mouse.

3	Day	Date	Start time	End time	Break	Work hours
4	Sun	10/1/2023	8:00	16:00	1:00	7:00
5	Mon	10/2/2023	8:00	16:00	1:00	
6	Tue	10/3/2023	8:00	17:30	1:00	

40. Double-click on the fill handle to automatically fill the following cells.
    Result: The formula is automatically to the cells below up to row 34.

18.3.12 Deleting weekends

41. Select cell C4 to F4 and all subsequent weekends. However, do not select the contents in columns A and B. Hold down the **control key** Ctrl to create multiple selections.

	A	B	C	D	E	F	G	H
1	**Work hours**							
2								
3	**Day**	**Date**	**Start time**	**End time**	**Break**	**Work hours**		
4	Sun	10/1/2023	8:00	16:00	1:00	7:00		
5	Mon	10/2/2023	8:00	16:00	1:00	7:00		
6	Tue	10/3/2023	8:00	17:30	1:00	8:30		
7	Wed	10/4/2023	8:00	18:21	1:00	9:21		
8	Thu	10/5/2023	8:00	16:00	1:00	7:00		
9	Fri	10/6/2023	8:00	16:00	1:00	7:00		
10	Sat	10/7/2023	8:00	16:00	1:00	7:00		
11	Sun	10/8/2023	8:00	16:00	1:00	7:00		
12	Mon	10/9/2023	8:00	16:30	1:00	7:30		
13	Tue	10/10/2023	8:00	16:00	1:00	7:00		
14	Wed	10/11/2023	8:00	14:37	1:00	5:37		
15	Thu	10/12/2023	8:00	19:08	1:00	10:08		
16	Fri	10/13/2023	8:00	16:00	1:00	7:00		
17	Sat	10/14/2023	8:00	16:00	1:00	7:00		
18	Sun	10/15/2023	8:00	16:00	1:00	7:00		
19	Mon	10/16/2023	8:00	15:30	1:00	6:30		
20	Tue	10/17/2023	8:00	16:06	1:00	7:06		
21	Wed	10/18/2023	8:00	16:00	1:00	7:00		
22	Thu	10/19/2023	8:00	16:00	1:00	7:00		
23	Fri	10/20/2023	8:00	17:15	1:00	8:15		
24	Sat	10/21/2023	8:00	16:00	1:00	7:00		
25	Sun	10/22/2023	8:00	16:00	1:00	7:00		
26	Mon	10/23/2023	8:00	18:15	1:00	9:15		
27	Tue	10/24/2023	8:00	16:00	1:00	7:00		
28	Wed	10/25/2023	8:00	19:00	1:00	10:00		
29	Thu	10/26/2023	8:00	16:00	1:00	7:00		
30	Fri	10/27/2023	8:00	20:00	1:00	11:00		
31	Sat	10/28/2023	8:00	16:00	1:00	7:00		
32	Sun	10/29/2023	8:00	16:00	1:00	7:00		
33	Mon	10/30/2023	8:00	16:00	1:00	7:00		
34	Tue	10/31/2023	8:00	16:00	1:00	7:00		
35								
36								

42. Press the **Delete key** Delete to delete the contents.

18.3.13 Highlighting the weekends

43. Select cells A6 to F6 and all subsequent weekends. Hold down the **control key** ⌈Ctrl⌉ to create multiple selections.

3	Day	Date	Start time	End time	Break	Work hours
4	Sun	10/1/2023					⬅
5	Mon	10/2/2023	8:00	16:00	1:00	7:00
6	Tue	10/3/2023	8:00	17:30	1:00	8:30
7	Wed	10/4/2023	8:00	18:21	1:00	9:21
8	Thu	10/5/2023	8:00	16:00	1:00	7:00
9	Fri	10/6/2023	8:00	16:00	1:00	7:00
10	Sat	10/7/2023					⬅
11	Sun	10/8/2023					
12	Mon	10/9/2023	8:00	16:30	1:00	7:30
13	Tue	10/10/2023	8:00	16:00	1:00	7:00
14	Wed	10/11/2023	8:00	14:37	1:00	5:37
15	Thu	10/12/2023	8:00	19:08	1:00	10:08
16	Fri	10/13/2023	8:00	16:00	1:00	7:00
17	Sat	10/14/2023					⬅
18	Sun	10/15/2023					
19	Mon	10/16/2023	8:00	15:30	1:00	6:30
20	Tue	10/17/2023	8:00	16:06	1:00	7:06
21	Wed	10/18/2023	8:00	16:00	1:00	7:00
22	Thu	10/19/2023	8:00	16:00	1:00	7:00
23	Fri	10/20/2023	8:00	17:15	1:00	8:15
24	Sat	10/21/2023					⬅
25	Sun	10/22/2023					
26	Mon	10/23/2023	8:00	18:15	1:00	9:15
27	Tue	10/24/2023	8:00	16:00	1:00	7:00
28	Wed	10/25/2023	8:00	19:00	1:00	10:00
29	Thu	10/26/2023	8:00	16:00	1:00	7:00
30	Fri	10/27/2023	8:00	20:00	1:00	11:00
31	Sat	10/28/2023					⬅
32	Sun	10/29/2023					
33	Mon	10/30/2023	8:00	16:00	1:00	7:00
34	Tue	10/31/2023	8:00	16:00	1:00	7:00

44. Format these areas with the fill color **Green, Accent 6, Lighter 60%**.

18.3.14 Border formatting

45. Select any cell in the range A3 to F34.
46. Press the keyboard shortcut **control key** ⌈Ctrl⌉ + ⌈A⌉ to select the entire table.

47. Format the cells with **All Borders** ⊞.

18.3.15 Displaying the results in the status bar

Sometimes values need to be calculated quickly without having to enter a formula. In the following example, you add up the times for a working week without entering a formula.

48. Select the cells F26 to F30 and look at the Excel *status bar* at the bottom right.

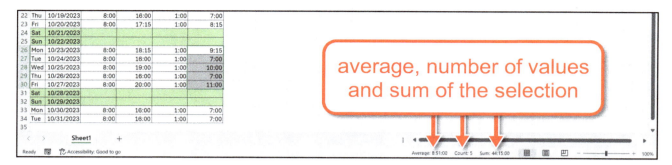

average, number of values and sum of the selection

Result: The average value, the number of values and the sum of the selected cells are displayed.

49. Add the numbers in your head to check the displayed sum.

18.3.16   Calculating the sum

50. Enter the word *Sum* in cell A35.

51. Select the cells F4 to F35 and click on the *AutoSum* button $\boxed{\Sigma}$ to calculate the sum of work hours for the month. Look at the result.

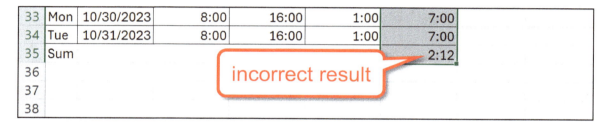

incorrect result

Result: The sum of cells F4 to F34 is calculated in cell F35. To do this, Excel automatically enters the formula *=SUM(F4:F34)*.

Advice: The formula is correct, but the displayed result is not. The reason for this is the current time format of cell F35. The used time format is a 24 hour clock format. It is not suitable for displaying added hours. It does not go beyond the time 23:59. After 23:59, this format displays 0:00 again and not 24:00 hours.

Example: 12:00 + 15:00 would be displayed as 3:00 and not as 27:00 hours.

18.3.17   Changing the time format

52. Select cell F35.

53. Click on the small arrow $\boxed{\searrow}$ at the bottom right of the *Number* group to open the *Format Cells* dialog box.

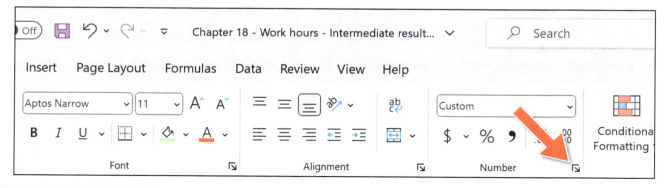

54. Click on the **Time** category to activate this category.

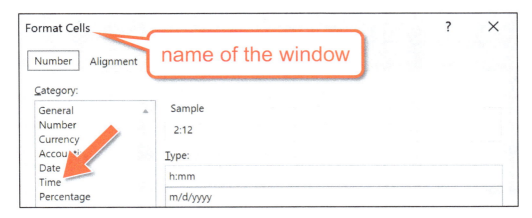

> **Advice:** The **Time** format also contains hour format variants and date + time combinations.

55. In the **Time** category, click on the entry **37:30:55** in the Type field.

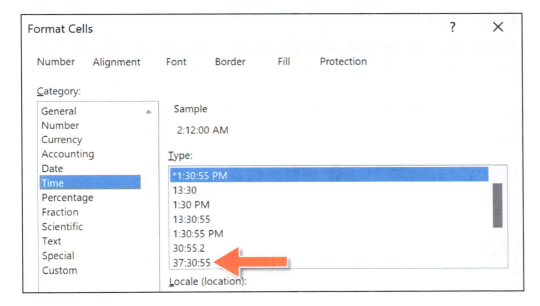

> **Advice:** The **37:30:55** format is an hourly format. It goes beyond the 24-hour rhythm. The value 37:30:55 results from:
> 24:00:00 + 13:30:55 = 37:30:55
> The value 13:30:55 is an arbitrary example time that Excel uses in the **Type** field.

56. Click on the **OK** button and look at the result.

> **Result:** The added hours are displayed correctly.

57. Format the cells A35 and F35 in bold.

18.3.18 Conclusion

58. Save the file and close Excel.

19   Instruction: Weddings

Use these instructions to calculate the estimated beverage requirements for a restaurant. The calculation is based on three wedding celebrations in January 2024.

19.1   New content

- order of operations using parentheses

19.2   Repetitions

- preventing automatic formatting using an apostrophe
- moving cells between other cells
- wrapping text inside a cell

19.3   Instruction

19.3.1   Opening the sample file

1. Open the sample file **Chapter 19 - Weddings - Start - B2** and enable editing.

19.3.2   Inserting a row

A new row is to be inserted above row 3.

2. Click on the row header of row 3 to select row 3.

	A	B	C
1	**Weddings**		
2	January 2024		
3			
4	**Family**	**Guests**	
5	Miller	180	
6	Johnson	74	
7	Alvez	143	
8			
9	**Item**	**Average per guest**	**Total**
10	Cola 7 fl oz	2	794
11	Lemonade 7 fl oz	1	397
12	Water 7 fl oz	2	794
13	Apple juice 7 fl oz	1	397
14	Orange juice 7 fl oz	1.5	595.5
15	Beer 10 fl oz	4	1588
16	Champagne 25 fl oz	0.3	119.1
17	Red wine 25 fl oz	0.1	39.7
18	White wine 25 fl oz	0.1	39.7
19			

Result: Weddings

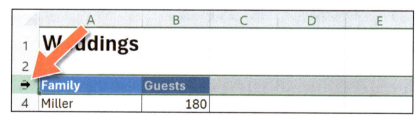

Advice: The black arrow ➡ is used to select a whole row.

3. Click on icon or the text of the **Insert** button [⊞ Insert ⌄]. However, do <u>not</u> click on the arrow [⌄] next to the button.

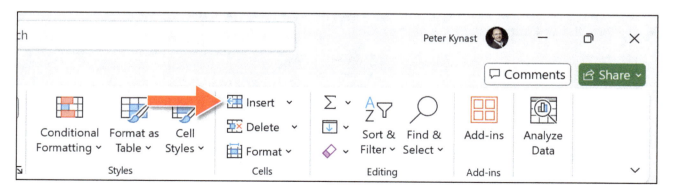

Result: A new row is inserted above the selected row.

Advice: The **Insert** button consists of two parts. The first part is the symbol and the label. The second part is a small arrow $\boxed{\vee}$. It is used to open the list box. If you click on the first part of the button (symbol and text), the **Insert** command is performed <u>directly</u>. A new row is inserted immediately. The basic rule here is that the number of rows inserted is always the same as the number of rows currently selected. Since an entire row is selected, an entire row is inserted. The new row adopts the formats of the row that was <u>above</u> the selected row before insertion.

19.3.3   Entering the month

The heading **January 2024** is to be entered in cell A2. An incorrect procedure is shown first to demonstrate a frequently occurring error.

4. Select cell A2 and look at the **Number Format** list box.

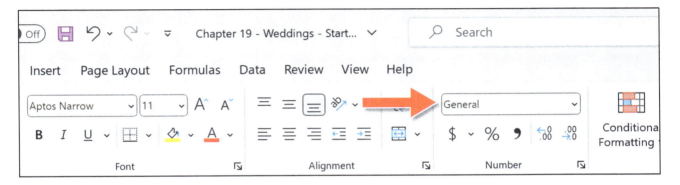

Advice: The **Number Format** list box indicates that cell A2 is formatted with the **General** number format. This is the default setting for all cells.

5. Enter the text **January 2024** in cell A2.

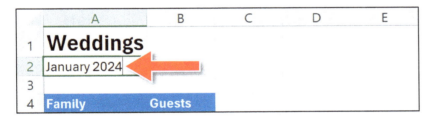

6. Confirm the entry and look at the result.

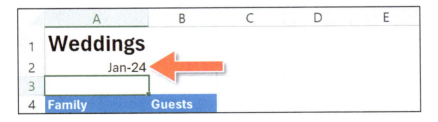

Result: The format is automatically changed when you confirm the entry. **January 2024** becomes **Jan-24**. The date was entered as text. However, when the entry is completed, this text is converted into a date. A date format is assigned to the cell. This format shortens the entry **January 2024** to **Jan-24**. This automatic formatting initially irritating. However, it can be easily prevented

19.3.4   Checking the number format

7. Select cell A2 and look at the **Number Format** list box.

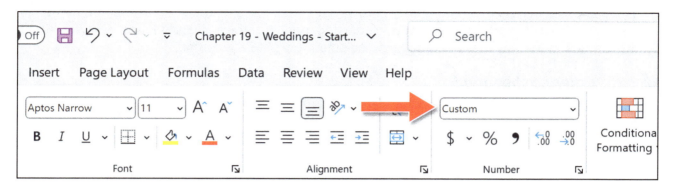

> **Result:** When the input was completed, the number format was automatically changed from **General** to **Custom**. In this case, **Custom** is a date format.

19.3.5   Correcting the number format

8. Enter the text **'January 2024** in A2. This will overwrite the old content.

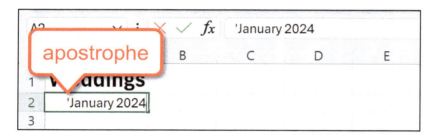

> **Advice:** Pay attention to the preceding apostrophe ('). You can insert the apostrophe using the **apostrophe key** next to the **enter key** .

9. Look at the result.

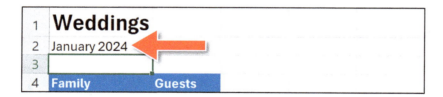

> **Result:** No more automatic changes are made. The apostrophe is not displayed.
> **Advice:** A preceding apostrophe prevents automatic changes to entries. It is not displayed, but it is part of the cell content.

19.3.6   Deleting a row

10. Click on the row header of row 9 to select row 9.

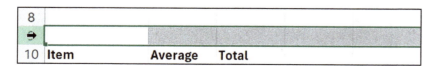

> **Advice:** The black arrow ➡ is used to select an entire row.

11. Click on the **Delete** button 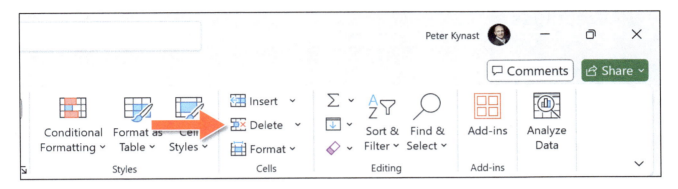 to delete the row. Do <u>not</u> click on the small arrow ⌄ next to the button.

Advice: The small arrow would open the list box for this button. Of course, you could also delete the row in this way. You would then click on the **Delete Sheet Rows** list item in the list box. In this situation, however, a different procedure for deleting rows is shown. Clicking the **Delete** button always deletes as many cells as are selected at that time! Since an entire row is selected, an entire row is also deleted.

19.3.7 Copying formats

Cells A9 to C9 should be assigned the same formats as cell A4. The formats can of course be set individually. However, this process can be simplified using the **Format Painter** tool. All formats are copied to the cells at the same time.

12. Select cell A4 and click on the **Format Painter** button.

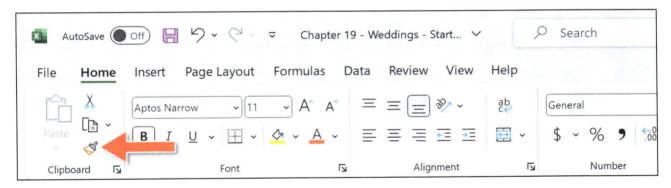

Result: The tool is activated and cell A4 is displayed with an animated frame.

Advice: The illustration above was created on a medium-sized screen. The **Format Painter** button is only displayed as an icon. On larger screens, the **Format Painter** button ⟨Format Painter⟩ is displayed with the corresponding name.

13. Point to any cell with the mouse. However, do not click on this cell.

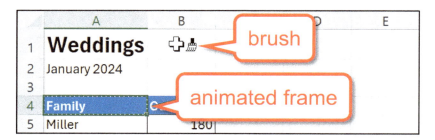

Result: A brush 🖌 is displayed next to the white cross ✚.
Advice: The brush symbolizes the active **Format Painter** function. Pointing means placing the mouse on a position without clicking.

14. Select cells A9 to C9 to copy the format to these cells.

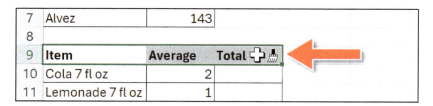

Result: When the mouse button is released, the format is copied to cells A9 to C9. The **Format Painter** function is deactivated again.

15. Look at the result. The formats are copied.

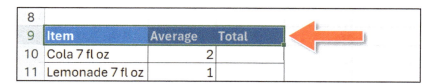

19.3.8   Wrapping text within a cell

16. Select B9 and press the **function key** F2 to activate edit mode.

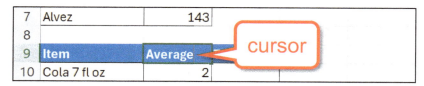

Result: The cursor is positioned after the word **Average**.

17. Press the keyboard shortcut Alt + **enter key** ↵ to create line break in the cell.

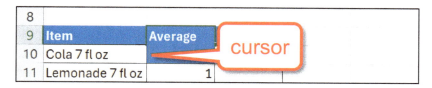

Advice: The entry is not completed by this key combination! Text wrap used to be called line break.
Read more: Please also read Chapter 26 Explanation: Keyboard shortcuts, page 146.

18. Enter the text **per guest** in the second line.

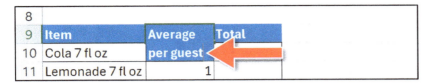

19. Press the **enter key** ⏎ to confirm the entry and look at the result.

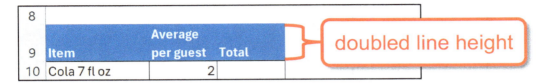

doubled line height

Result: The input is completed. The height of row 9 is doubled. It automatically adjusts to the content of cell B9.

19.3.9   Checking the text wrap

20. Select cell B9 and look at the **Wrap Text** button ⎁.

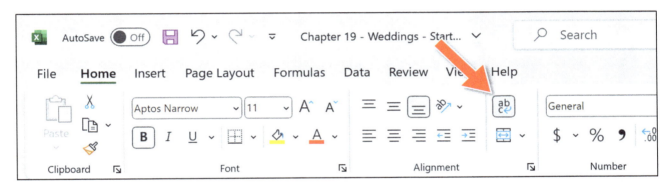

Advice: The grey background of the button symbolizes that this format is active for the selected cell. The text wrap was generated by the keyboard shortcut Alt + **enter key** ⏎ and has changed the format of the cell. Text wrap used to be called line break in earlier versions of Excel.

19.3.10   Using parentheses to alter the order of operations

The restaurant is planning the drinks order for January 2024. Weddings are being organized for three families. 397 visitors are registered for the three celebrations (B5+B6+B7). The restaurant calculates an average value of drinks per guest based on the experience of recent years. Cells B10 to B18 contain these empirical values. The total quantities for purchasing should be calculated in column C. To demonstrate the importance of the parentheses, these are initially omitted. This results in an incorrect calculation.

21. Enter the formula **=B5+B6+B7*B10** in cell C10.

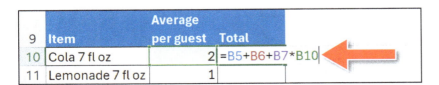

Advice: This formula is incorrect! It is intended to show that parentheses are necessary to obtain the correct result.

22. Confirm the entry and look at the result.

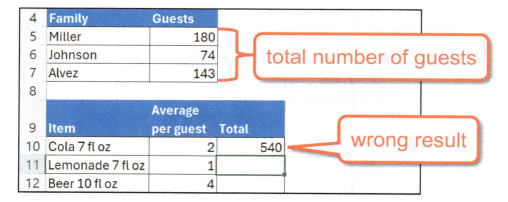

Result: The result of the formula is incorrect!

Advice: A total of 397 guests are expected (180 + 74 + 143 = 397). This value must be multiplied by the number 2 (B10). The correct result is therefore **794**. The result 540 is displayed because Excel follows the order of operations called **PEMDAS** (**P**arentheses, **E**xponents, **M**ultiplication, **D**ivision, **A**ddition, **S**ubtraction)! No parentheses have been set, therefore the multiplication of B7 and B10 has priority over the additions. The current (incorrect) calculation reads:

Step 1: 143 * 2 = 286

Step 2: 286 + 180 + 74 = 540

To add up the total number of guests first, the additions must be placed in parentheses. Only then can the multiplication be carried out.

23. Select C10 and press the **function key** $\boxed{\text{F2}}$ to activate edit mode.

24. Add the parentheses to the formula **=(B5+B6+B7)*B10**.

9	Item	Average per guest	Total
10	Cola 7 fl oz	2	=(B5+B6+B7)*B10
11	Lemonade 7 fl oz	1	

Advice: First, the total number of guests must be determined. Then, this total is multiplied by the average quantity per guest. Excel follows the order of operations called **PEMDAS**. Arithmetic operations containing multiplications and divisions are prioritized over additions and subtractions. Parentheses can be used to change the order of these calculations.

25. Confirm the entry. The correct result is displayed.

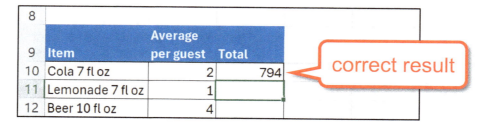

Advice: The dollar signs are still missing, because the references to B5, B6 and B7 must not change when using the formula to fill the cells below. This error is shown in the following steps.

26. Select cell C10 and double-click the fill handle to copy the formula to the cells below.

9	Item	Average per guest	Total	
10	Cola 7 fl oz	2	794	
11	Lemonade 7 fl oz	1		

27. Look at the result. Incorrect results are displayed.

9	Item	Average per guest	Total
10	Cola 7 fl oz	2	794
11	Lemonade 7 fl oz	1	217
12	Beer 10 fl oz	4	#VALUE!
13	Water 7 fl oz	2	#VALUE!
14	Apple juice 7 fl oz	1	#VALUE!
15	Orange juice 7 fl o	1.5	10.5
16	Champagne 25 fl	0.3	2.1
17	Red wine 25 fl oz	0.1	0.7
18	White wine 25 fl o	0.1	0.45

incorrect results

28. Select cells C11 and activate edit mode.

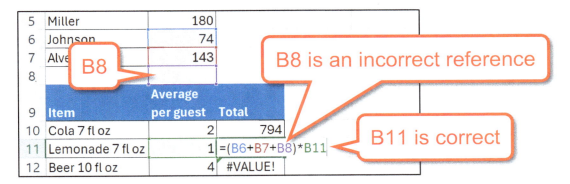

5	Miller	180	
6	Johnson	74	
7	Alve	143	
8			

B8

B8 is an incorrect reference

9	Item	Average per guest	Total
10	Cola 7 fl oz	2	794
11	Lemonade 7 fl oz	1	=(B6+B7+B8)*B11
12	Beer 10 fl oz	4	#VALUE!

B11 is correct

Result: The row details of all references are changed. B5 becomes B6, B6 becomes B7 and B7 becomes B8. However, only the change from B10 to B11 is desired.

29. Exit edit mode and change the formula in C10 to *=(B$5+B$6+B$+7)*B10*.

30. Confirm the entry and copy the formula to cells C11 to C18.

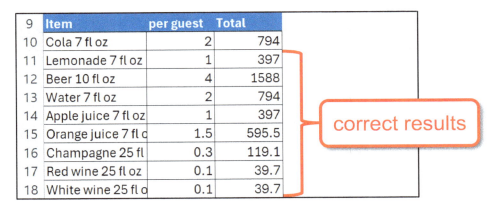

9	Item	per guest	Total
10	Cola 7 fl oz	2	794
11	Lemonade 7 fl oz	1	397
12	Beer 10 fl oz	4	1588
13	Water 7 fl oz	2	794
14	Apple juice 7 fl oz	1	397
15	Orange juice 7 fl o	1.5	595.5
16	Champagne 25 fl	0.3	119.1
17	Red wine 25 fl oz	0.1	39.7
18	White wine 25 fl o	0.1	39.7

correct results

19.3.11 Moving rows between other rows

Row 12 (beer) should be moved to the other alcoholic beverages.

31. Select A12 to C12 and point to the border of the cell pointer with the mouse.

11	Lemonade 7 fl oz	1	397
12	Beer 10 fl oz	4	1588
13	Water 7 fl oz	2	794
14	Apple juice 7 fl oz	1	397

32. Press and hold the **shift key** ⇧ .

33. Hold down the **shift key** ⇧ and drag the mouse between rows 15 and 16. Pay attention to the green line and the tooltip.

11	Lemonade 7 fl oz	1	
12	Beer 10 fl oz	4	
13	Water 7 fl oz	2	
14	Apple juice 7 fl oz	1	
15	Orange juice 7 fl oz	1.5	595.5
16	Champagne 25 fl	0.3	119.1
17	Red wine 25 fl oz		39.7

green line

tooltip

A16:C16

Result: The green line and the tooltip (A16:C16) indicate the new position. Make sure that the green line is displayed <u>horizontally</u> as in the illustration above.

Attention: If the green line is displayed vertically as in the following illustration, the mouse is too far away from the center of the cell. In this case, move the mouse further towards the center of the cell.

14	Apple juice 7 fl oz	1	397
	7 fl d	1.5	595.5
	e 25 fl	B15:D15 0.3	119.1
17	Red wine 25 fl oz	0.1	39.7

wrong

34. First release the mouse button and then the **shift key** ⇧ .

Advice: This order is crucial. If you were to release the shift key first, you would move the cells to the other cells. However, the aim is to place the cells <u>between</u> the other cells.

35. Look at the result.

13	Apple juice 7 fl oz	1	397
14	Orange juice 7 fl d	1.5	595.5
15	Beer 10 fl oz	4	1588
16	Champagne 25 fl	0.3	119.1
17	Red wine 25 fl oz	0.1	39.7

Result: The beer row is inserted between orange juice and champagne.

36. Adjust the width of column A to fit the content **Champagne 25 fl oz** of cell A16 without cutting off.

19.3.12 Conclusion

37. Save the file and close Excel.

20   Instruction: Employees

Use these instructions to calculate the number of employees in a company.

20.1   New content

- sorting data
- sum of area and a single cell

20.2   Repetitions

- Moving cells
- Inserting several columns
- Selecting related areas quickly
- unmerging cells
- AutoSum
- quick addition using the status bar

Result: Employees

20.3   Instruction

20.3.1   Opening the sample file

1. Open the sample file **Chapter 20 - Employees - Start - B2** and enable editing.

20.3.2   Checking and correcting errors

A common error is described below. Cell A3 contains descriptive text and number (number of employees). Cells B3 and C3 are empty. At first glance, however, it looks as if the two cells have content.

2. Select cell C3 and look at the formula bar.

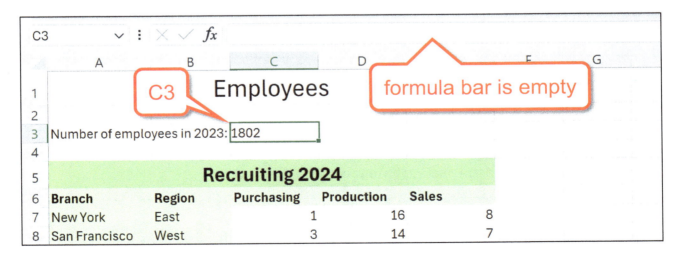

Result: The formula bar is empty. C3 has no content.
Advice: The whole text <u>and</u> the number 1802 are the content of cell A3. However, if the text and number are in the same cell, this cell cannot be used for calculations. The data must be separated.

3. Select cell A3 and look at the formula bar.

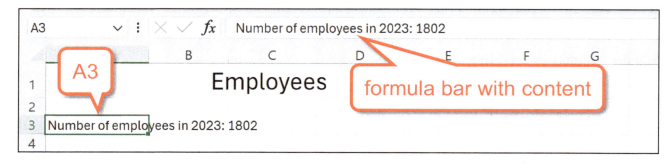

Result: The formula displays the content of A3.

4. Press the **function key** F2 to activate edit mode.
5. Delete the number *1802* from this cell.

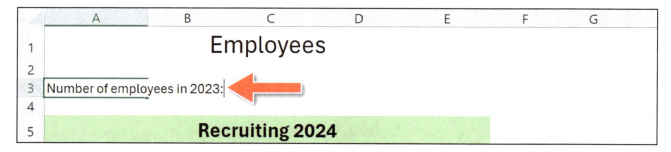

6. Confirm the entry.
7. Enter the number of employees *1802* in D3.

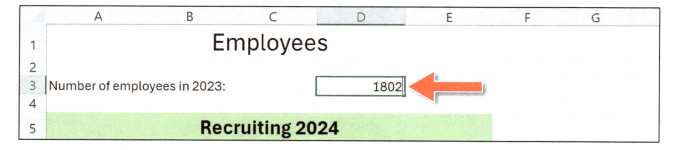

20.3.3   *Inserting two columns*

Two columns will be inserted before column D. As the insertion of columns has already been done, a different method is shown this time.

8. Click on the column header of column D and, while holding down the left mouse button, drag the mouse to column header E to select these two columns.

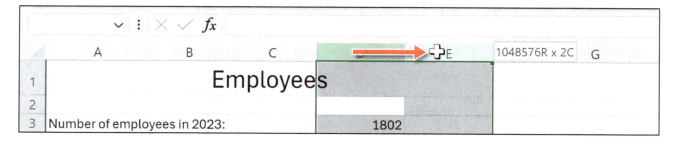

9. Click on icon or the text of the **Insert** button 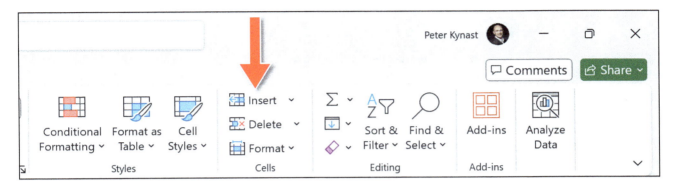. However, do <u>not</u> click on the arrow next to the button.

Result: Two columns are inserted before column D. The new columns adopt the formats of the column to the left of the selection (column C).

Advice: Cells are inserted immediately when the **Insert** button is clicked. Exactly as many cells are always inserted as are currently selected. In this situation, two whole columns are selected, so two whole columns are also inserted.

20.3.4   Moving cells

10. Select cell F3 and point to the edge of the cell with the mouse. However, do not place the mouse on the fill handle.

11. Move cell F3 to C3 this time.

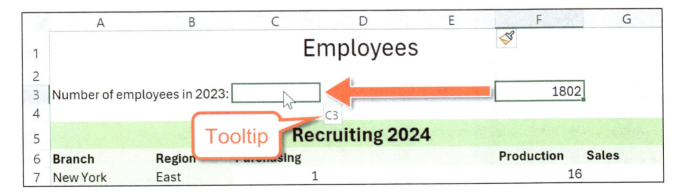

Advice: If the number had been entered in C3 instead of D3 before, it would not have been moved by inserting new columns. This was done to show how Excel handles inserting columns.

20.3.5   Data entry

12. Add the following data into the two new columns.

	Branch	Region	Purchasing	Warehouse	Service	Production	Sales
4							
5			**Recruiting 2024**				
6	**Branch**	**Region**	**Purchasing**	**Warehouse**	**Service**	**Production**	**Sales**
7	New York	East	1	5	2	16	8
8	San Francisco	West	3	4	4	14	7
9	Philadelphia	East	1	3	2	10	3
10	Billings	North	1	4	1	14	4
11	Washington	East	3	2	7	16	6
12	Las Vegas	West	2	5	2	9	8
13	Austin	South	1	3	5	17	4
14	Sacramento	West	1	2	3	13	8
15	Houston	South	3	1	5	18	6
16	Boston	East	2	2	1	12	5
17							

20.3.6   Determining the employees per location

13. Select the area C7 to H16.

	Branch	Region	Purchasing	Warehouse	Service	Production	Sales	
5			**Recruiting 2024**					
6	**Branch**	**Region**	**Purchasing**	**Warehouse**	**Service**	**Production**	**Sales**	
7	New York	East	1	5	2	16	8	
8	San Francisco	West	3	4	4	14	7	
9	Philadelphia	East	1	3	2	10	3	
10	Billings	North	1	4	1	14	4	
11	Washington	East	3	2	7	16	6	←
12	Las Vegas	West	2	5	2	9	8	
13	Austin	South	1	3	5	17	4	
14	Sacramento	West	1	2	3	13	8	
15	Houston	South	3	1	5	18	6	
16	Boston	East	2	2	1	12	5	
17								

14. Click on the **AutoSum** button Σ to calculate the sums.
    Result: The sums are inserted in cells H7 to H16.
15. Enter the heading **Sums** in cell H6.
    Result: The formatting is automatically adopted.
    Advice: Many formats are set automatically if they have already been used three times without interruption. They are then automatically added to the cell when a new entry is made in this row. The entry can be made directly next to the formatted area or two cells apart.

20.3.7   Merge & Center cells

16. Select A1 to H1 and click on the **Merge & Center** button to unmerge the cells.
    Result: The current cells are split into their respective cells. The selection remains unchanged.

17. Click on the **Merge & Center** button again.
    Result: The second click merges and centers the cells and the content again.

18. Look at the result.

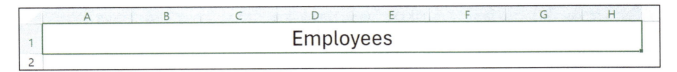

19. Correct the connection of the cells in row 5 in the same way.

20.3.8 Formatting borders

20. Select any cell in the area A5 to H16.
21. Press the keyboard shortcut **control key** `Ctrl` + `A` to select the related area.

	Branch	Region	Purchasing	Warehouse	Service	Production	Sales	Sums
5	Recruiting 2024							
6	Branch	Region	Purchasing	Warehouse	Service	Production	Sales	Sums
7	New York	East	1	5	2	16	8	32
8	San Francisco	West	3	4	4	14	7	32
9	Philadelphia	East	1	3	2	10	3	19
10	Billings	North	1	4	1	14	4	24
11	Washington	East	3	2	7	16	6	34
12	Las Vegas	West	2	5	2	9	8	26
13	Austin	South	1	3	5	17	4	30
14	Sacramento	West	1	2	3	13	8	27
15	Houston	South	3	1	5	18	6	33
16	Boston	East	2	2	1	12	5	22

22. Format this area with **All Borders** ⊞.

20.3.9 Calculating the total number of employees

23. Enter the formula **=SUM(H7:H16,C3)** in cell C18.

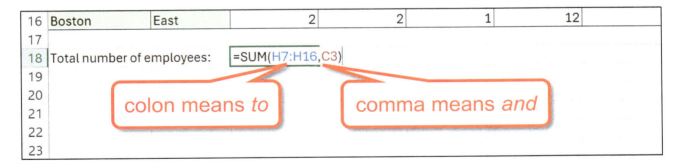

Advice: This notation means: Add the cells from H7 to H16 <u>and</u> the cell C3. Cell references and names of functions are written in capital letters by default. However, you can also use lower case. Excel automatically converts the letters to upper case when you confirm the entry.
Or: The formulas **=SUM(H7:H16)+C3** and **=C3+SUM(H7:H16)** are equivalent.

20.3.10 Sorting data

The data should be sorted by city in ascending order. First, the corresponding column is selected with the cell pointer. The subsequent sorting is based on the selected column.

24. Select any cell in the cell range A7 to A16 (column A).

	Branch	Region	Purchasing	Warehouse	Service	Production	Sales
6	**Branch**	**Region**	**Purchasing**	**Warehouse**	**Service**	**Production**	**Sales**
7	New York	East	1	5	2	16	
8	San Francisco	West		4	4	14	
9	Philadelphia	East		3	2	10	
10	Billings	North	1	4	1	14	
11	Washington	East	3	2	7	16	

cell pointer

Advice: The cell pointer selects a column. Sorting is based on this column.

25. Click on the **Sort & Filter** button to open the list box.

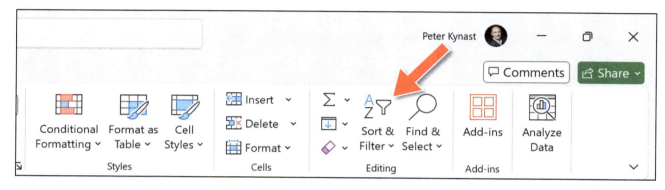

26. Click on the **Sort A to Z** list item.

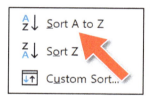

Result: The data is sorted by city name in ascending order.

27. Look at the result and check the sorting.

	Branch	Region	Purchasing	Warehouse	Service	Production	Sales	Sums
4								
5				**Recruiting 2024**				
6	**Branch**	**Region**	**Purchasing**	**Warehouse**	**Service**	**Production**	**Sales**	**Sums**
7	Austin	South	1	3	5	17	4	30
8	Billings	North	1	4	1	14	4	24
9	Boston	East	2	2	1	12	5	22
10	Houston	South		1	5	18	6	33
11	Las Vegas	West				9	8	26
12	New York	East				16	8	32
13	Philadelphia	East	1		2	10	3	19
14	Sacramento	West	1	2	3	13	8	27
15	San Francisco	West	3	4	4	14	7	32
16	Washington	East	3	2	7	16	6	34
17								

cities sorted in ascending

Advice: Excel sorts by <u>whole</u> rows by default. This avoids errors. The related data in the rows remain together.

28. Also check the values that belong to the cities.
    Advice: You can check the values in their original sorting order in step 21.
29. Select any cell in the cell range B7 to B16 (regions) and sort the data in descending order (Sort Z to A). Look at the result.

	Branch	Region	Purchasing	Warehouse	Service	Production	Sales	Sums
2								
3	Number of employees in 2023:		1802					
4								
5	**Recruiting 2024**							
6	**Branch**	**Region**	**Purchasing**	**Warehouse**	**Service**	**Production**	**Sales**	**Sums**
7	Las Vegas	West	2	5	2	9	8	26
8	Sacramento	West	1	2	3	13	8	27
9	San Francisco	West	3	4	4	14	7	32
10	Austin	South	1	3	5	17	4	30
11	Houston	South						33
12	Billings	North						24
13	Boston	East	2	2	1	12	3	22
14	New York	East	1	5	2	16	8	32
15	Philadelphia	East	1	3	2	10	3	19
16	Washington	East	3	2	7	16	6	34
17								
18	Total number of employees:		2081					
19								

regions sorted in descending order

20.3.11 Displaying the results in the status bar

Sometimes you want to calculate figures without the result appearing in the table. The total number of new employees in this year is calculated using the status bar below.

30. Select the cells H7 to H16 and look at the status bar.

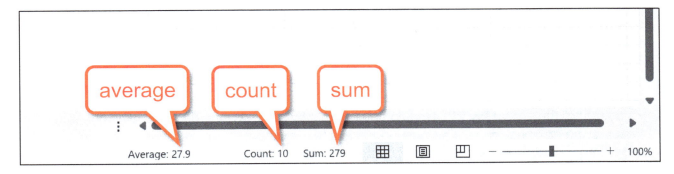

average   count   sum

Average: 27.9   Count: 10   Sum: 279   100%

Result: The average value, the number and the sum of the selected values (H7 to H16) are displayed in the status bar. This display disappears again as soon as you deselect the values.

20.3.12 Conclusion

31. Save the file and close Excel.

21   Instruction: Currency conversion

Use these instructions to convert various currencies into dollar.

21.1   New content

- correcting number alignment

21.2   Repetitions

- generating number and month series
- deleting dollar format
- removing fill colors
- correcting formulas

21.3   Instruction

21.3.1   Opening the sample file

1. Open the sample file **Chapter 21 - Currency conversion - Start - B2** and enable editing.

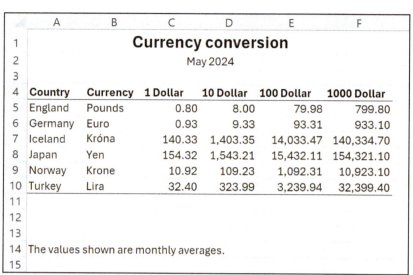

	A	B	C	D	E	F
1			**Currency conversion**			
2			May 2024			
3						
4	**Country**	**Currency**	**1 Dollar**	**10 Dollar**	**100 Dollar**	**1000 Dollar**
5	England	Pounds	0.80	8.00	79.98	799.80
6	Germany	Euro	0.93	9.33	93.31	933.10
7	Iceland	Króna	140.33	1,403.35	14,033.47	140,334.70
8	Japan	Yen	154.32	1,543.21	15,432.11	154,321.10
9	Norway	Krone	10.92	109.23	1,092.31	10,923.10
10	Turkey	Lira	32.40	323.99	3,239.94	32,399.40
11						
12						
13						
14	The values shown are monthly averages.					
15						

Result: Currency conversion

21.3.2   Preventing automatic formatting

2. Enter the text **'May 2024** in cell A2. Pay attention to the preceding apostrophe (').

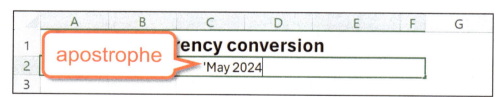

Advice: You can insert the apostrophe by pressing the **apostrophe key** ⌨ next to the **enter key** ↵. Using the **accent key** ⌨ will not work as intended. If you enter the date without the apostrophe, the entry **May 2024** would be replaced by **May-24**. The entry remains unchanged if you enter it with an apostrophe. The cell content is a text! Without the apostrophe, Excel converts the entry into a date. In this case, the cell content would not be text, but a number formatted as a date.

3. Confirm the entry and look at the result.

Result: The input is not changes. The apostrophe (') is not visible. However, it is part of the cell content. When editing the cell, the apostrophe becomes visible again.

21.3.3   Number signs (#)

Number signs have a protective function in Excel. Sometimes columns are too narrow and the numbers inside cannot be displayed in full. However, numbers must never be cut off. In these cases, the numbers are replaced by number signs. The number signs prevent the display and printing of incomplete and incorrect numbers.

4. Set the column width for column F to **8.43**. The value is displayed as a tooltip when dragging.

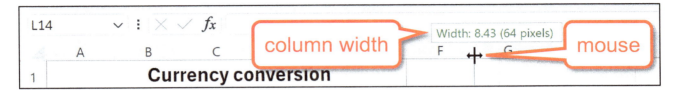

Result: All numbers in column D are readable again.
Advice: 8.43 is the standard width of all columns. The width is specified in two units. The first unit is characters. The column width 8.43 means that 8.43 standard characters can be displayed next to each other. The second unit is pixels.

21.3.4 Using the pointing method with the keyboard

The currency amounts for 1000 dollars are to be determined in column E. Formulas can be entered manually or by using the pointing method. The pointing method can in turn be used by mouse click or keyboard.

5. Enter an equal sign (=) in cell E5.

4	Country	Currency	1 Dollar	100 Dollar	1000 Dollar	10 Dollar
5	England	Pounds	0.7998	79.98	=	
6	Norway	Krone	10.9231	1092.31		109.231

6. Press the **left arrow** key ← once.

4	Country	Currency	1 Dollar	100 Dollar	1000 Dollar	10 Dollar
5	England	Pounds	0.7998	79.98	=D5	
6	Norway	Krone	10.9231	1092.31		
7	Turkey	Lira	32.3994	3239.94		323.994

cell reference D5

Result: The cell reference D5 is entered into the formula. Cell D5 is highlighted with an animated frame.

7. Press the **left arrow** key ← again.

4	Country	Currency	1 Dollar	100 Dollar	1000 Dollar	10 Dollar
5	England	Pounds	0.7998	79.98	=C5	
6	Norway	Krone	10.9231	1092.31		
7	Turkey	Lira	32.3994	3239.94		323.994

cell reference D5

Result: The animated frame is set to cell C5. The corresponding cell reference is displayed in the formula.

8. Complete the formula as follows: **=C5*1000** and confirm the entry.

4	Country	Currency	1 Dollar	100 Dollar	1000 Dollar	10 Dollar
5	England	Pounds	0.7998	79.98	=C5*1000	98
6	Norway	Krone	10.9231	1092.31		109.231

21.3.5   Auto Fill Options - Copy without formatting

When filling cells, the cell contents and formats are copied. In many cases, however, copying the formats is not desired. You can use the **Auto Fill Options** button to decide whether you only want to copy the formats or only the content.

9. Copy the formula in E5 to cells E6 to E10.
10. Undo the selection and look at the result.

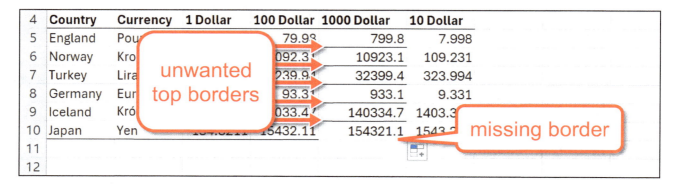

Advice: Before filling, cell E5 only had the **Top Border** formatting. This border was copied to the subsequent cells. However, E5 did not have a border at the bottom. Therefore, this border is missing in cell E10 after filling the cells. No alignment is set for cell C5.

11. Click on the **Auto Fill Options** button 📋 to open the list box for this button.

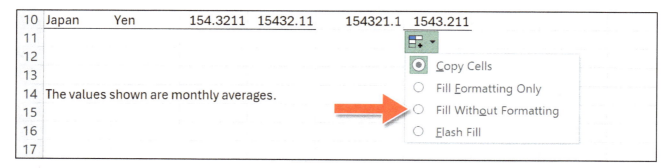

12. Click on the list item **Fill Without Formatting**.

10	Japan	Yen	154.3211	15432.11	154321.1	1543.211
11						
12						
13						
14	The values shown are monthly averages.					
15						
16						
17						

- Copy Cells
- Fill Formatting Only
- Fill Without Formatting
- Flash Fill

Result: The incorrect borders are removed again. Only the formula is copied.

21.3.6   Moving columns between other columns

Column F is sorted incorrectly. It should be placed between columns C and D.

13. Select the cell range F4 to F10.

14. Point to the border of the cell pointer. Do <u>not</u> point to the fill handle.

3						
4	**Country**	**Currency**	**1 Dollar**	**100 Dollar**	**1000 Dollar**	**10 Dollar**
5	England	Pounds	0.7998	79.98	799.8	7.998
6	Norway	Krone			0923.1	109.231
7	Turkey	Lira	cross with 4 arrows		399.4	323.994
8	Germany	Euro			933.1	9.331
9	Iceland	Króna	140.3347	14033.47	140334.7	1403.347
10	Japan	Yen	154.3211	15432.11	154321.1	1543.211
11						
12						

Result: The mouse pointer is displayed with a cross consisting of four arrows.

15. Press and hold the **shift key** ⇧.

16. Hold down the **shift key** ⇧ and drag the mouse to the left between columns C and D. Pay attention to the position of the green line.

3						
4	**Country**	**Currency**	**1 Dollar**	**100 Dollar**	**1000 Dollar**	**10 Dollar**
5	England		7998	79.98	799.8	7.998
6	Norway	green line	9231	1092.31		109.231
7	Turkey		3994	D4:D10	mouse	323.994
8	Germany	Euro	0.9331	93.31		9.331
9	Iceland	Króna	140.3347	14033.47	140334.7	1403.347
10	Japan	Yen	154.3211	15432.11	154321.1	1543.211
11						
12						

Advice: The green line indicates the new position of the cells. It must be placed as shown in the illustration. This process requires a little practice. If you have accidentally inserted the cells in the wrong place, click on the **Undo** button ↺ and carry out the process again.

17. First release the mouse button and then the **shift key** ⇧.

   Result: Column F is placed between column C and D.

   Advice: This order is crucial. If you were to release the shift key first, you would move the cells <u>onto</u> and not between the other cells.

18. Undo the selection and look at the result. The order of the values is sorted correctly: $ 1, $ 10, $ 100 and $ 1000.

3						
4	**Country**	**Currency**	**1 Dollar**	**10 Dollar**	**100 Dollar**	**1000 Dollar**
5	England	Pounds	0.7998	7.998	79.98	799.8

Advice: The set column widths are not moved! The heading in Column F is now slightly cut off and column E is too wide.

19. Set the column width of column E to **10 (75 pixel)**.

20. Set the column width of column F to **11 (82 pixel)**.

21.3.7   Decreasing decimal places

All amounts should be shown with two decimal places and the thousands separator, but without the dollar sign.

21. Select the cells C5 to F10.

22. Click on the small arrow ▣ at the bottom right of the **Number** group to open the **Format Cells** dialog box.

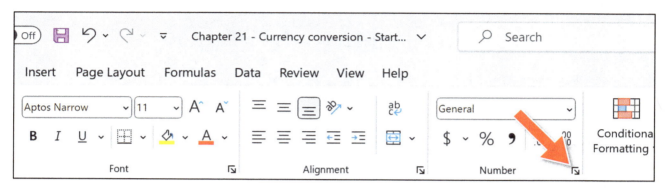

23. Click on the **Number** category to activate this category.

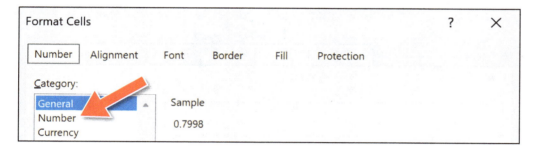

    Result: The settings for this category are displayed.

24. Open the **Fill Color** list box and click on **No Fill** to remove the white fill color.

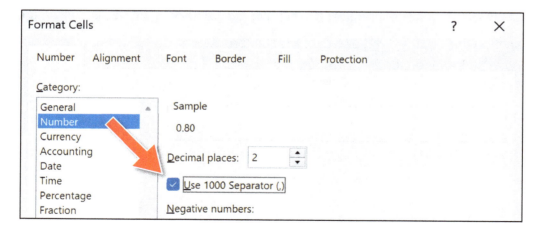

    Advice: Two decimal places are automatically preset.

25. Click on the **OK** button to save the setting.

21.3.8   Sorting

The currencies should be sorted by country in ascending order.

26. Select any cell in the range from A5 to A10.

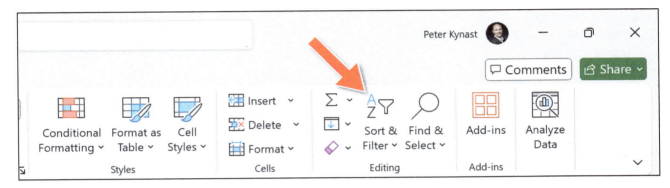

5	England	Pounds	0.80	8.00	79.98	799.80
6	Norway	Kr...	109.23	1,092.31	10,923.10
7	Turkey	Lira	323.99	3,239.94	32,399.40
8	Germany	Euro	0.93	9.33	93.31	933.10
9	Iceland	Króna	140.33	1,403.35	14,033.47	140,334.70
10	Japan	Yen	154.32	1,543.21	15,432.11	154,321.10

Advice: Use the cell pointer to select a column. The subsequent sorting is based on this column.

27. Click on the **Sort & Filter** button to open this list box.

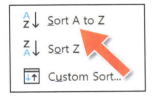

28. Click on the **Sort A to Z** list item to sort the data in ascending order.

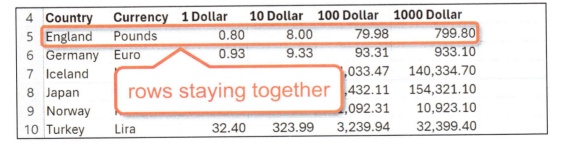

Result: The data is sorted <u>row by row</u> by country in ascending order.
Advice: Rows must <u>always</u> remain tougher when sorting. If only cells A5 to A10 were sorted. The data would be distorted.

29. Check the data. Ensure that the sorting is correct.

4	**Country**	**Currency**	**1 Dollar**	**10 Dollar**	**100 Dollar**	**1000 Dollar**
5	England	Pounds	0.80	8.00	79.98	799.80
6	Germany	Euro	0.93	9.33	93.31	933.10
7	Iceland				,033.47	140,334.70
8	Japan				,432.11	154,321.10
9	Norway				,092.31	10,923.10
10	Turkey	Lira	32.40	323.99	3,239.94	32,399.40

Advice: When sorting, the rows remain together. The data is sorted by country. The associated currency and values are also sorted.

21.3.9   Conclusion

30. Save the file and close Excel.

22   Exercise: Devices

This exercise serves as a learning check and is the conclusion of the fourth section. Unlike instructions, the solution is not described here. You can see an illustration of the finished table on the right side.

22.1   Contents

- preventing automatic formatting
- correcting number formats
- wrapping text in a cell
- filling several cells at the same time
- moving cell areas between cells
- sorting data
- sum of two areas

22.2   Exercise

1. Open the sample file **Chapter 22 - Devices - Start - B2** and enable editing.
2. Enter the date **September 2023** in cell A3. The date should not change automatically to **Sep 23**.
3. Enter the word **printer** in cells A7, A13 and A19 <u>at the same time</u>. To do this, use the **control key** to create a selection of A7, A13 and A19 and complete the entry of the word **printer** with the keyboard shortcut **control key + enter key**.

	A	B	C	D	E
1	**Devices**				
2	September 2023				
3					
4	**Computers and devices**	**Brooklyn**	**Detroit**	**Memphis**	**New York**
5	Computer	7	5	4	17
6	Copier	2	2	1	3
7	Printer	2	2	1	3
8	Sums	11	9	6	23
9					
10	**Computers and devices**	**Omaha**	**Orlando**	**Salem**	**Tampa**
11	Computer	9	12	8	23
12	Copier	1	2	3	2
13	Printer	2	7	1	4
14	Sums	12	21	12	29
15					
16	**Evaluation**	**Sums**			
17	Computer	85			
18	Copier	16			
19	Printer	22			
20	Sum	123			
21					

Result: Devices

4. Correct the number formats in cells D11 and E13. Simple numbers should be displayed. There are 3 copiers in Salem and 4 printers in Tampa.
5. Enter the text **Computers and devices** in cells A4 and A10. Insert a line break after the term **Computers**.
6. Center the names of the cities vertically.
7. The cities should also be sorted alphabetically. Move the column for **Detroit** between **Brooklyn** and **Memphis**.
8. Format all three tables with all borders with the border color **Orange, Accent 2, Darker 50%**.
9. Sort all three tables alphabetically in ascending order by device name.
10. Calculate the sum of the computers in cell B17. All eight cities should be added together. To do this, create a SUM function that adds both ranges.
11. Copy the formula from B17 to cells B18 and B19.
12. Calculate the sum of all devices in cell B20.
13. Save the file and close Excel.

Section 5

Explanations

Contents of this section:

- functions
- contents and formats
- cell references
- keyboard shortcuts

23 Explanation: Functions

23.1 Formulas and functions

There are formulas with and without functions. Functions are commands in a formula. Typical functions are SUM, MIN, MAX and AVERAGE.

23.1.1 Examples of formulas without functions

=A1+A2   =A1-A2   =A1*A2   =A1/A2

23.1.2 Examples of formulas with functions

=SUM(A1:A10)   =MAX(A1:A10)   =A1-SUM(A2:A10)   =SUM(A1:A10,A20)

Functions are used to simplify calculation steps. Many evaluations are also only possible with a function, e.g. determining the largest value (MAX function). The largest value cannot be determined using basic arithmetic operations alone.

23.2 Syntax

All functions have a defined notation. This notation is also called **syntax**. When entering a function, this syntax is displayed in a tooltip. The tooltip appears as soon as you enter the left parenthesis.

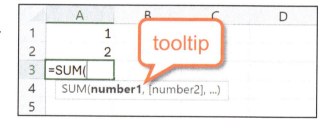

In the illustration on the right, the tooltip shows the following notation for the SUM function:

SUM(number1, [number2], …)

The opening equal sign is not displayed in the tooltip. It is not part of the function. It belongs to the formula and only appears once at the beginning of each formula. The terms **number1** and **number2** may be misleading. The following syntax might be more understandable:

SUM(range)

This is the way in which the SUM function is most frequently used. The cells in a certain area are summed up (added).

23.2.1 Further examples

Formula	Explanation
=SUM(A1:A10)-SUM(D1:D10)	Subtracts an area from another area.
=SUM(A1:A10,D1:D10)	Adds two areas.
=MAX(A1:A10,D1:D10)	Determines the largest value from two areas.
=AVERAGE(A1:A10,D1:D10)	Calculates the average of two areas.
=SUM(A1:A10,D1)	Adds an area and a single cell.
=MIN(A1:A10,D1)	Determines the smallest value from a range and a single cell.

In the following books you will get to know more functions.

24   Explanation: Contents and formats

The display of a cell is always a combination of its content <u>and</u> its format.

24.1   Contents

The content of a cell is either a **text**, a **number** or a **formula**. These are the most important types of content. Other types will be introduced in subsequent books.

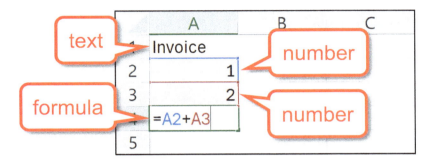

24.2   Formats

A distinction is made between the following formats: Cell formats, column formats, row formats and formats for entire worksheet and pages. Format means property. It determines the appearance or display of a cell, row, column or worksheet.

24.2.1   Cell formats

The cell format is the most important format. It is divided into the following categories. Numbers, alignment, font, frame, fill and protection. These categories appear as tabs in the **Format Cells** dialog box.

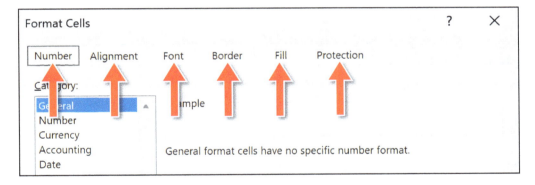

Category	Examples
Number	General, currency, date, time, percentage, fraction, custom etc.
Alignment	Align left, align right, centered, top, centered across selection, distributed, etc.
Font	Font, font size, font color, underline, strikethrough, bold, italic, superscript, etc.
Border	All borders, different border colors, line styles, line thicknesses, diagonal, etc.
Fill	Background color of the cell (fill color), background patterns/gradients (fill effects), etc.
Protection	Cells can be locked for editing. The settings **Protect Sheet** <u>and</u> **Protect Workbook** in the **Review** tab must be active for this feature to work properly.

25   Explanation: Cell references

Excel distinguishes between relative, mixed and absolute references. Relative references are automatically changed when copying formulas. This applies to filling cells with the black cross as well. The terms copying and filling are synonymous.

If a change in the references is not desired, a mixed or absolute reference must be used. Mixed and absolute references are created by adding a dollar sign ($). This character prevents a reference from being changed when copying or filling in formulas. The dollar sign is always placed <u>before</u> the part of the reference (letter or number) that is not to be changed.

Reference	Description	Explanation
A1	relative reference	Both the letter and the number can be changed when copying formulas. Which part of a reference is changed depends on whether the formula is copied vertically or horizontally. In Excel Part 1, you only worked with relative references.
$A1	mixed reference, absolute row reference	When copying a formula horizontally, Excel would change the letters of the references. However, the A is anchored (fixed) by the dollar sign ($). A is <u>not</u> changed.
A$1	Mixed reference, absolute column reference	When copying a formula vertically, Excel would change the numbers of the references. However, the 1 is anchored (fixed) by the dollar sign ($). The 1 is <u>not</u> changed.
A1	absolute reference, absolute column <u>and</u> row reference	Both parts of the reference are fixed. Regardless of whether you copy the formula vertically or horizontally. There is no change with an absolute reference. This part of Excel book series does not yet contain any formulas with absolute references. However, they are mentioned here for the sake of completeness.

25.1   Relative references

Advice: When copying vertically, the number of the cell reference per row are changed by the value 1.

Advice: When copying horizontally, the letters of the cell references per column are changed by one place in the alphabet.

25.1.1   *Example of copying formulas vertically with relative references*

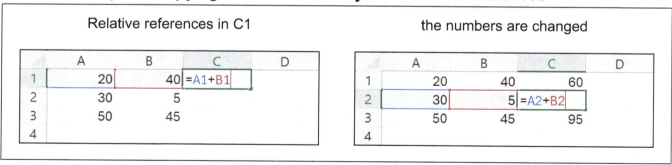

25.1.2   *Example of copying formulas horizontally with relative references*

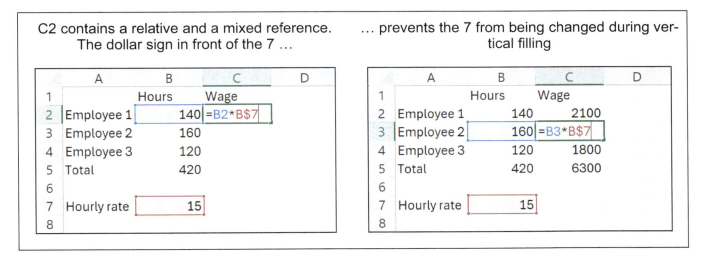

25.2   Mixed references

If a cell reference is <u>not</u> to be changed during copying, a mixed or absolute reference must be created. Mixed and absolute references are created by adding dollar signs.

Advice: If a formula with mixed or absolute references is copied, the letters and numbers remain unchanged if a dollar sign is entered <u>in front of them</u>.

	A	B	C	D
1		Hours	Wage	
2	Employee 1	140	=B2*B$7	
3	Employee 2	160		
4	Employee 3	120		
5	Total	420		
6				
7	Hourly rate	15		
8				

C2 contains a relative and a mixed reference. The dollar sign in front of the 7 …

	A	B	C	D
1		Hours	Wage	
2	Employee 1	140	2100	
3	Employee 2	160	=B3*B$7	
4	Employee 3	120	1800	
5	Total	420	6300	
6				
7	Hourly rate	15		
8				

… prevents the 7 from being changed during vertical filling

Attention: If you were to copy the formula **=B2*B$7** horizontally, <u>both</u> letters would be changed because there is no dollar sign in front of either letter. Of course, copying the formula horizontally in this tables makes no sense. This note is only intended to improve understanding.

26   Explanation: Keyboard shortcuts

The following table contains keyboard shortcuts for Excel. These are single keys and key combinations. A key combination consists of two or three keys. The following applies to all key combinations: Hold down the first key or the first two keys and briefly press the last key. Then release the first button(s) again.

Example: You want to press the key combination **control key** [Ctrl] + [F4]. To do this, hold down the **control key** [Ctrl] and briefly press the **function key** [F4]. Then release the **control key** [Ctrl] again.

No.	Function	Key(s)	Description
1.	Help	[F1]	Displays the Excel Help task pane.
2.	Edit mode	[F2]	Activates edit mode.
3.	Repeat last action	[F4]	Repeats the last action, e.g. formatting. However, this does not apply to all actions. For example, the **function key** [F4] does not repeat any entries
4.	Anchoring (fixing) cell, inserting dollar sign	[F4]	In edit mode, cell references can be set using the **function key** [F4]. The cursor must be positioned at the corresponding reference. Pressing F4 creates the different reference types one after the other.
5.	Removing cell contents	[Delete]	Removes the cell contents. The formats are retained! They may have to be deleted separately.
6.	Fill the selected cell range	[Ctrl] + [↵]	Automatically fills the selected area. 1. Select cells 2. Make an entry in the active cell 3. Press the **control key** [Ctrl] + **enter key** [↵]
7.	Selecting the related area	[Ctrl] + [A]	Selects the related table area in which the cell pointer is located.
8.	Creating text wrap (line break) inside a cell	[Alt] + [↵]	Ends a line within a cell. But does not close the input.

Attention: The keyboards of laptops often differ from the keyboards of stand-alone devices (desktop PCs). On desktop PC keyboards, the function keys ([F1] to [F12]) almost always have only one assignment. On laptops, these keys often have two <u>functions</u>. On many laptops, for example, the F1 key also has the function **Reduce volume** or the function **Reduce screen brightness**. Unfortunately, it is not possible to make a general statement on this. The manufacturers of the devices decide this very differently. However, the following usually applies: The second function of a key is activated on laptops or smaller keyboards by <u>additionally</u> pressing the **Fn key** [Fn]. The Fn key is usually located at the bottom left of the laptop keyboard. Try out the setting on your device.

27   Index

You can use this list to look up terms and topics. For ease of use, some content is stored with multiple keywords.

www.ingramcontent.com/pod-product-compliance
Lightning Source LLC
LaVergne TN
LVHW081757050326

832903LV00027B/1985